Online!

**A Reference Guide to
Using Internet Sources**

1998 Edition

Contents

8 Using CBE Style to Cite and Document Sources *123*

9 Observing Netiquette *135*

Preface

In the twelve months since *Online!* was first published, we've been simply overwhelmed by the response. Clearly, students and teachers alike have many questions about using Internet sources — and we're happy to have provided some answers:

- Help accessing and evaluating Internet sources
- Models for citing and documenting Internet sources in the MLA, APA, CBE, and *Chicago* styles
- Tips for communicating and publishing on the Internet and the World Wide Web
- A directory of Internet sources in the major academic disciplines

We're pleased now to offer this 1998 update of *Online!* This edition has been updated thoroughly to reflect changes in the Internet and its use.

New to the 1998 edition

New features you'll find in this edition of *Online!* include the following:

- 1998 MLA guidelines for citing Web sources, reflecting the newly introduced citation style of the Modern Language Association of America
- A new chapter on netiquette, giving answers to the most frequently asked questions about the conventions of communicating in the various Internet venues

- A new chapter on the principles of Web-page design, showing teachers and students how to compose effectively in webbed environments

- A sensational new *Online!* Web site, now much easier to navigate and reflecting the principles of our own chapter on Web page design—visit us at <http://www.smpcollege.com/online-4styles~help>

This book was born in early 1996 when we found ourselves unable to provide good answers to our students' questions about citing and documenting Internet sources. After reading everything we could find on using the Internet for research purposes and examining every documentation style sheet and manual available, we drafted a set of guidelines for citing Internet sources MLA-style and presented them at several professional conferences in Kentucky. We then published "Beyond the *MLA Handbook*: Documenting Electronic Sources on the Internet" in *Kairos: A Journal for Teaching Writing in Webbed Environments* 1.2 (1996) at <http://eng.ttu.edu/kairos/1.2/inbox/mla.html>. That essay identified four areas of citation practice needing improvement and offered an MLA-style guide. Within days, our email boxes were flooded with requests for permission to reprint and distribute these guidelines. Enter Edith Trost, from St. Martin's Press, who asked whether we would consider expanding our essay into a textbook. We would indeed—and *Online! A Reference Guide to Using Internet Sources* was born. Since then, the Modern Language Association has written its own official style for citing Internet sources, and we're pleased to present official MLA style now (in Chapter 5). We're especially pleased to be part of an ongoing—indeed, an expanding—scholarly conversation about documentation and its important implications.

We've tried to make *Online!* the latest word on working with Internet sources—but we know that it's the latest word as of December 1997. And we know as well that it won't be long before new kinds of Internet sources emerge, bringing new questions. Take those questions to our site on the World Wide Web at <http://www.bedfordstmartins.com/online>. We hope this site, and this book, will be practical and useful—helpful harbors for all who navigate the Internet.

Acknowledgments

To all who have helped us prepare *Online!* we give our thanks and appreciation. We especially want to acknowledge the help of Mick Doherty, the editor of *Kairos*, for encouraging us to publish the initial essay, and Janice Walker, for her generous response to that essay. We gratefully salute the staff of Eastern Kentucky University's Academic Computing and Telecommunications Services, especially Margaret Lane and Melvin Alcorn, for their abundant and generous assistance along the way. We say thanks to all the students in Honors Rhetoric who have asked great questions about the Internet. We acknowledge all who created and subscribe to the Alliance for Computers and Writing for sustaining one of the world's most informative and helpful listservs. We are grateful to Cindy Tallis-Wright, MOO teacher extraordinaire at Diversity University, and to Joe Pellegrino, a superb webmaster and colleague who graciously reviewed Chapter 10 and helped improve it substantially for this edition.

For this 1998 edition, we benefited from the astute suggestions of the following reviewers, to whom we say thanks upon thanks: Suzanne Auldridge, University of Colorado at Denver; Anne Bliss, University of Colorado at Boulder; Isabel L. Danforth, Wethersfield (Connecticut) Public Library; James J. Dent, Sam Houston State University; Bradley A. Hammer, Ohio State University; Susan M. Herdrick, Spokane State University; Ronald L. Higgins, Keene State University; Charles Hill, University of Wisconsin at Oshkosh; Claudine Keenan, Pennsylvania State University at Allentown; David Lapides, University of Texas at Austin; Thomas Lowderbaugh, Smithsonian Institute and University of Maryland; Kathleen Murphey, Community College of Philadelphia; Lolly Smith, Everett Community College; and Pamela Yenser and the Report Writing students at Eastern Oregon State University.

From the Bluegrass of Kentucky we bow eastward in deep gratitude to Marilyn Moller, Carla Samodulski, and especially Talvi Laev—our wonderful and able Park Avenue South editors whom we've come to know so well as friends and as the best of readers. Finally, we hug and cheer our families—our wives, Paula and Beth, and our children, Chelsea, Amy, Lisa, Kirk, Jonathan, and

Benjamin, all of whom gave us the love, encouragement, and time to begin and complete *Online!* To all, a thousand thanks!

Andrew Harnack
<engharnack@acs.eku.edu>

Eugene Kleppinger
<actklepp@acs.eku.edu>

Glossary

This glossary appears at the beginning of *Online!* because understanding the language of the Internet is crucial to your use of this book. This language includes technical terms, jargon, and even slang, and some of it may be quite new to you. If you have little or no experience using the Internet for research, take some time to read through the glossary now. Later, as you come across terms or concepts that need clarification, you'll find help here.

You'll encounter many of these terms again and again as you use the Internet — and as you use *Online!* To make the book easy to use, all the terms in the glossary are highlighted when they're introduced in the text; whenever you come across a highlighted word, know that you'll find it explained in the glossary.

To learn more about topics covered in the glossary, visit the *Online!* homepage at <http://www.smpcollege.com/online-4styles~help>.

< > (angle brackets)   Angle brackets around text indicate that all the characters within the brackets must be treated as a single unit, with no spaces between parts, as in <http://www.infolink.org/glossary.htm>. By using angle brackets to frame handwritten or printed electronic information (e.g., email addresses and Web site locations), you prevent misinterpretation. Leave the angle brackets off such information when you type it into your browser's or email program's dialog box.

@ (the "at" sign)   A fixture in every email address, @ separates the username from the domain name, indicating that you are "at" a particular electronic

1

address. For example, <jhsmith@acs.eku.edu> indicates that someone, possibly Jane Smith, gets email at Academic Computing Services, which is at Eastern Kentucky University, an educational institution. See also *email* and *email address*.

. (the dot) The period symbol, called "the dot" in online lingo, is used to separate parts of email addresses, URLs, and newsgroup names, as in <jhsmith@acs.eku.edu>, <http://www.yahoo.com>, and <alt.sci.ecology>.

/ (the forward slash) Used to separate parts of URLs, as in <ftp://ftp.tidbits.com/pub>; not to be confused with the backward slash \ used in DOS directory paths.

> (the greater-than sign) A symbol used in email messages to indicate text that is being quoted from a previous message. Most email programs automatically mark quoted text this way.

account name See *username*.

address book Your collection of email addresses.

Archie An Internet search tool for finding and retrieving computer files from archives.

archive A collection of computer files stored on a server. FTP sites are typical examples of archives.

article Internet lingo for a message posted online.

ASCII An acronym for American Standard Code for Information Interchange, ASCII is the most basic format for transferring files between different programs. It is sometimes referred to in wordprocessing programs as "unformatted text."

asynchronous communication Electronic communication involving messages that are posted and received at different times. Email is an example of such delayed communication.

attachment A file, such as a spreadsheet or word-processed document, sent along with an email message.

BBS (bulletin board service) A service maintained by a computer that serves as an information hub for many computers. People with common interests subscribe to a BBS in order to post and receive messages.

bookmark (n.) An entry in a bookmark list.

bookmark (v.) To use your browser's menu to save a bookmark.

bookmark list A browser's pull-down menu or pop-up window containing links to Web sites you want to visit frequently; sometimes called a *hotlist*.

browser A computer program for navigating the Internet. Most browsers display graphics and formatted pages and let you click on hyperlinks to "jump" from one Web page to another. Widely used *graphic browsers* include HotJava, Microsoft Internet Explorer, NCSA Mosaic, and Netscape Navigator. A popular *text-only browser* is Lynx.

bulletin board service See *BBS*.

channel A virtual meeting place for groups or private IRCs, usually with a set topic of conversation.

click-and-hold To hold down a Macintosh mouse button (e.g., over a link or inside a frame) to open the context menu.

client A requester of information. As you surf the Internet, you, your computer, or your browser may be considered an Internet client.

context menu A pop-up menu giving choices related to the cursor's position inside a window, opened by right-clicking the mouse (in Windows) or click-and-holding (on a Macintosh). Context menus often provide features not obtainable from a program's ordinary menu bar. The context menu for a hyperlink, for example, lets you save or bookmark that item without visiting it.

cyber- A prefix describing something that has been created electronically and is available online (e.g., a *cyberworld*, a *cybercity*, a *cyberstore*). *Cyber* can also stand alone as an adjective, especially to avoid clunky compounds: *cyber rights, cyber cowboy, cyber pipe dreams*.

cyberography See *webliography*.

cyberspace The Internet; more loosely, the online world.

dialog box A window on your computer screen that prompts you to make choices or confirm a command to let a program continue, or a box into which you can type something. After you type your input, submit it by pressing the Enter key or clicking an onscreen button.

digital Electronic; *wired.*

digital watermark Ownership information embedded in a graphics file and used to trace unauthorized downloading and use of images.

direct access A computer connection that lets you use Internet software (e.g., a graphic browser) on your personal computer.

directory A list or collection of related computer files, sometimes called a *folder.* A directory may contain other directories, which are then called *subdirectories.*

directory path The sequence of directories and subdirectories you need to open to find a particular computer file. For example, the directory path <pub \data\history> shows that the *history* file is in the *data* subdirectory, which in turn is in the *pub* directory.

domain See *domain name.*

domain name The string of letters and symbols associated with a Web site or email service provider, as in <www.enigmacom.com>. A domain name has at least two *elements* (parts), separated by periods. The first element or elements uniquely identify an organization's server, while the final element, called the *domain,* identifies the type of organization operating the server. Common suffixes include *.com* (commercial), *.edu* (educational), *.gov* (government), *.mil* (military), *.net* (network management), and *.org* (non-commercial/nonprofit). Domains outside the United States often identify the country in which a server is located (e.g., *.au* for Australia, *.ch* for Switzerland).

download To transfer information electronically from one computer to another, as when you move a program from an archive to your computer.

ejournal (electronic journal) A journal, popular or scholarly, published primarily on the Internet.

email (electronic mail) Any of various programs that send and receive messages over a network.

email address The address you use to send and receive email. Your email address contains your username, the @ symbol, and the domain name, as in <jhsmith@acs.eku.edu>.

emoticons Small graphic renderings, composed of ASCII characters, that writers substitute for facial expressions and body language. Emoticons are useful in an online world where curt or hastily written messages can easily offend, and where you may want to indicate humor, surprise, or some other emotion to readers who cannot see you. Some of the most popular emoticons are :-) (smile), :-((frown), :-/ (skeptical), }:-> (devilish), and :-o (surprised). For a fuller list, see *Internet Smileys* at <http://members.aol.com/bearpage/smileys.htm>.

ezine (electronic magazine) A magazine published primarily on the Internet

FAQ (frequently asked questions) Pronounced "eff-ay-cue" or "fack"; a file containing answers to common questions that new users of a program or service might ask. If you are new to a newsgroup or listserv, look up the group's FAQ file and read the answers to questions others have already asked.

favorite A bookmark in Microsoft Internet Explorer. See also *bookmark (n.)*.

flame A personal attack on someone, usually within a listserv or newsgroup thread.

frame A distinct part of a Web page, with its own scroll bars. Links in one frame often control the display in other frames on the same page.

FTP (file transfer protocol) The set of commands used to transfer files between computers on the Internet.

GIF (graphics interchange format) Pronounced "jiff" or "giff"; one of two common formats (the other is JPEG) for image files associated with Web documents. The acronym appears at the end of the filename, as in <marsface.gif>.

gopher A program for accessing Internet information through hierarchical menus, gopher will "go for" the information you select and will display it on your screen. When you use gopher through direct access, with a graphic browser, you choose menu items by clicking your computer's mouse. When you use gopher through indirect access, the menu lists choices by line number, and you select what you want using keyboard commands. Gopher's text-oriented file format makes it especially useful for searching large collections of texts such as electronic books, library catalogs, historical documents, and specialized databases. On the World Wide Web, gopher addresses begin with *gopher://* instead of *http://*.

header The area in an email message that contains routing information—who sent the message, where the message originated, the date it was sent, the route it took, and so on.

history list A list (usually a pull-down menu) of the Web pages you most recently visited. History lists let you return quickly to a site or see an overview of your latest surfing session.

hit In Internet lingo, hit can mean (1) an item in the list of search results a browser gives you ("AltaVista's search for *scorpions* turned up sixty-nine hits"), or (2) accessing of a Web page by an Internet surfer ("The *Online!* Web page received three dozen hits this week").

homepage Usually the first page you see when you access a particular Web site, a homepage has hypertext links to other pages on the same server or to other Web servers.

hotlink See *hyperlink*.

hotlist See *bookmark list*.

HTML (hypertext markup language) A computer code that allows you to create pages on the World Wide Web. HTML "tags" electronic text to indicate how it should be displayed onscreen by browsers. It provides a common language for browsers using different computer systems (Mac, PC, Unix, etc.).

HTTP (hypertext transfer protocol) The communication rules used by browsers and servers to move HTML documents across the Web.

hyperlink A connection between two places on the Web. Hyperlinks are represented onscreen by highlighted icons or text. Selecting a hyperlink makes your browser "jump" from one place to another. Hyperlinks are sometimes called *hotlinks*.

HyperNews See *Web discussion forum*.

hypertext A document coded in HTML; a collection of such documents.

hypertext link A connection between two documents or sections of a document on the Web; a type of *hyperlink*.

hypertext markup language See *HTML*.

hypertext transfer protocol See *HTTP*.

image map An image containing clickable links to other Web documents.

indirect access A computer connection that lets you run Internet programs stored on another computer system; also called *shell access.*

Internet A vast network of computers offering many types of services, including email and access to the World Wide Web. As a "network of networks," the Internet links computers around the world.

Internet relay chat See *IRC.*

Internet service provider (ISP) A person or company providing access to the Internet.

IRC (Internet relay chat) The online equivalent of CB radio and telephone conferencing, IRC lets you communicate synchronously (in "real time") with other people. See also *real-time communication.*

ISP See *Internet service provider.*

JPEG (Joint Photographic Experts Group) Pronounced "jay-peg"; one of two common formats (the other is GIF) for image files associated with Web documents. In filenames the acronym appears as *jpeg* or *jpg,* as in <pluto.jpg>.

keyword The term you type into a search tool's dialog box; what you want to search for.

linkage data Information about the hypertext context in which a document is located (i.e., the document's links to other documents).

listowner The person responsible for maintaining and/or monitoring a listserv.

listserv An ongoing email discussion about a technical or nontechnical issue. Participants subscribe via a central service, and listservs may have a moderator who manages information flow and content. (LIST-SERV is software licensed by L-Soft International, Inc., for management of electronic mailing lists. Similar products include ListProc, from the Corporation for Research and Educational Marketing, and Majordomo, distributed through <http://www.greatcircle.com>.)

lurk To watch or read without participating. Lurking on a listserv, for example, means that you read other people's messages but don't post messages yourself.

metaengine A Web search tool that combines results from several independent searches.

modem Equipment that connects a computer to a data transmission line (usually a telephone line), enabling the computer to communicate with other computers and the Internet.

moderator The person who reads all messages sent to a moderated newsgroup and decides whether a particular message is appropriate for posting.

MOO (multi-user domain, object-oriented) An electronic "space" in which many people can interact simultaneously. Accessible through telnet, MOOs enable classes, seminars, and friends to meet at a given time, usually to discuss a given topic.

MUD (multi-user domain) As electronic "spaces" for simultaneous communication, MUDs provide opportunities for role-playing in which each participant usually controls one character who has a complete life history and persona and can express a variety of physical and emotional responses.

netiquette A combination of the words *Net* and *etiquette, netiquette* refers to appropriate behavior on a network, and specifically on the Internet.

netizen Any person using the Internet.

newbie Someone new to the Internet; a beginner.

newsgroup A group of people and their collection of postings on the Usenet network. Newsgroups are open forums in which anyone may participate. Each newsgroup has a topic, which can be as broad as the focus of <alt.activism> or as narrow as the computer applications discusssed in <comp.sys.mac.apps>. See also *Usenet.*

online On a network; on the Internet.

password A personal code you use to access your computer account and keep it private.

pixel Shorthand for *picture element;* the smallest visible colored or monochrome dot a computer monitor can display.

plug-in Add-on software to increase a browser's capabilities.

post To send a message to someone online. An online message is a *posting.*

protocol A set of commands—the "language"—that computers use to exchange information. Often-used protocols include FTP, gopher, HTTP, mailto, and telnet.

real-time communication Electronic communication in which people converse simultaneously with one another; also called *synchronous communication*. MOOs, MUDs, and IRCs are examples of real-time communication.

right-click To use the right-side mouse button in Windows to open the context menu, which contains special functions for saving files and bookmarking. In Macintosh systems, you click-and-hold to open the context menu.

search engine See *search tool*.

search tool Any of various programs that work with your browser to find information on the Web. After you type a keyword or keywords into your browser's dialog box, a search tool looks for Web pages containing your keyword(s) and produces a menu of available documents (hits). Also called *search engine*.

server A computer or program that handles requests from client computers for data, email, file transfer, and other network services.

shell access See *indirect access*.

signature (sig) file A text and/or graphics file appended to your email and other postings. Signature files generally contain a name, an offline contact address, and sometimes a quotation or pithy saying.

snail mail The U.S. Postal Service or another agency that delivers messages by courier.

spam To fill someone's email with unwanted material (e.g., junk email).

subject directory A hypertext list of available Web sites categorized by subject; what you get when you use search tools such as Yahoo! or The Argus Clearinghouse.

subject guide See *webliography*.

subject line The title of a message as it appears in an email directory.

surf To navigate the Internet. A *surfer* is an avid Internet user.

synchronous communication See *real-time communication*.

TCP/IP An abbreviation for *transmission control protocol/Internet protocol*, TCP/IP controls software applications on the Internet.

teleport To "transport" a person or object electronically across a virtual space. In MOOs, characters and objects can be teleported instantaneously from one location to another.

telnet A program that lets you log onto another computer from your own computer using a username and a password.

text index A hypertext list of Web sites containing the keyword(s) you specify; what you get when you use search tools such as Lycos or AltaVista.

thread A series of postings about a particular topic. For example, you might decide to follow a *fire ants* thread in the newsgroup <alt.sci.ecology>.

thumbnail A miniature rendering of an image; used on the Web as a link to the full-sized version.

URL (uniform resource locator) Pronounced "you-are-ell." A string of characters that uniquely identifies each page of information on the World Wide Web; a Web address. The URL for *Online!* is <http://www.smpcollege.com/online-4styles~help>.

Usenet A network providing access to electronic discussion groups (newsgroups). You can join any of thousands of Usenet newsgroups by using a newsreader program.

Usenet newsgroup See *newsgroup*.

username The information that, combined with your password, lets you access your computer account; also called *account name, userid*. Your Internet email address probably begins with your username.

Veronica An acronym for Very Easy Rodent-Oriented Net-Wide Index to Computerized Archives. Veronica is a program that searches for files over all available gopher servers on the Internet.

virtual Online; occurring or existing in cyberspace.

WAIS (Wide Area Information Server) A program that searches a variety of Internet databases by looking for specific keywords in documents rather than simply looking at document titles.

Web See *World Wide Web*.

Web browser See *browser*.

Web discussion forum A Web page offering articles to read and giving readers special tools for responding online to articles and responses already posted by others. In HyperNews, one popular discussion format, all contributions are automatically added to the Web page, whose topically arranged menu gives convenient access to *threads* (ongoing discussions on specific topics).

Web site Any location on the World Wide Web.

webfolio A collection of a student's texts published for review on the Web. Writing instructors teaching online often ask students to submit webfolios instead of printed portfolios. Businesses, craftspeople, and artists create webfolios to display their products, services, and artwork.

webliography (1) An electronic bibliography (also called a *cyberography*); (2) a Web site linking many Internet resources for a specific topic (also called a *subject guide*).

wired Electronic; online.

wizard (1) An administrator of a MOO; (2) a feature included in some programs that provides step-by-step guidance to help users perform tasks.

World Wide Web (WWW) A global Internet service connecting hypertext data and resources. Using a browser, you can move quickly from one Web site to another in search of information, graphics, and data.

To find out more about Internet terms, visit the *Online!* Web site or consult the following Web resources:

ILC Glossary of Internet Terms
<http://www.matisse.net/files/glossary.html>

Netdictionary
<http://www.netdictionary.com>

Whatis.com
<http://whatis.com>

Wired Style
<http://www.hotwired.com/hardwired/wiredstyle>

CHAPTER ONE

Finding Internet Sources

You've probably seen the photograph from the 1997 Mars *Pathfinder* mission showing the rover *Sojourner* doing a "wheelie" on a rock nicknamed Yogi. Pictures of the Martian landscape became commonplace in the media during late 1997 as *Pathfinder* and *Sojourner* gave us exciting new perspectives on the geography, chemistry, and meteorology of a faraway planet.

If you wanted to know more about the *Pathfinder* mission, you might begin with print sources—NASA press releases, science magazines, news periodicals, and so on. You could interview a local astronomer or visit a planetarium. If you had access to *Pathfinder*'s photography archives on CD-ROM (and if you had the necessary viewing equipment), you could see the *Pathfinder* images for yourself.

Or you could turn to the Internet.

On the **Internet**, you could visit . . .

The official Mars *Pathfinder* Mission **homepage** at <http://wwwmpf.jpl.nasa.gov>

The Mars exploration page from *Astronomy Now* magazine at <http://www.astronomynow.com/mars>

The *Whole Mars Catalog* at <http://www.reston.com/astro/mars>

From these sites you could print a copy of an official photograph (see Figure 1.1), read relevant press releases, find more NASA data, and create a list of sources for future use.

The Internet became closely associated with the *Pathfinder* mission because NASA agreed to distribute photographs through these Web sites in "real time" (as soon as the data were received). Live-video news briefings and group discussions were available to anyone

Figure 1.1
Sojourner, Pathfinder's rover, contacts Yogi, a Martian rock, on July 10, 1997
<http://mars.sgi.com/ops/81314_full.jpg>

with an Internet connection. Computer storage of the pictures at many Internet locations created instant archives that remain readily accessible.

Besides viewing *Pathfinder's* photography and reading about the mission, you could use the Internet to consult with experts around the world by participating in online discussions about space exploration. You could locate and even join astronomy groups, whether local or distant. In short, Internet sources offer a virtual grab bag of sources. This book will help you sort out the ones that will be useful for you.

Doing research on the Internet brings new opportunities—and new challenges. The Internet is *democratic:* all voices have an equal chance to be heard. The Internet is *global:* you can read an online document published anywhere in the world. The Internet is *up-to-the-minute:* facts and figures can be as fresh as the second you request them. The Internet is *interactive,* promoting communication as intimate as personal email and as public as online journals and Internet conferencing. Best of all, the Internet is *free:* the information found there costs absolutely nothing. (You may have to pay for access to the Internet, but most of the files you find are free.)

Because Internet publishing is at once democratic, inexpensive, global, and instantaneous (and because it often bypasses the formalities of print publishing), you need to be concerned about the reliability of what you discover there. Helping you evaluate the reliability of Internet sources is one of the goals of this book. (See Chapter 4.)

1a Understanding the Internet

The Internet—sometimes simply called the Net—links computers around the world. When you're connected to the Internet, you can communicate with people, schools, organizations, governments, businesses—anyone who has a computer with an Internet connection. In cyberspace—the electronic world you go to when you communicate with others by computer—you can listen to distant radio broadcasts, watch movie clips, play chess around the clock with someone in Russia, send email to a friend in South America, chat with colleagues every Tuesday evening, do research on any topic imaginable, contact manufacturers' hotlines—even shop for a used car.

Box 1.1
Visiting the Internet

World Wide Web Use this resource to find information and do research.

email (electronic mail) Use this option to send and receive messages on the Internet.

Web discussion forums Visit these to read and respond to articles posted for specific audiences.

listservs Subscribe to these email services to join ongoing discussions on specific topics.

newsgroups Visit these to read and post messages to specific communities of people.

real-time communication Use MOOs, MUDs, and other "live" forums to converse with others and attend online classes and conferences.

telnet Use this protocol to log onto another computer from your own computer.

FTP (file transfer protocol) Use this protocol to transfer information from another computer to your own computer.

gopher Use this service's menus to find Internet sources.

So when you think of the Internet, think big. Imagine the Net as the communications mall of the world, a place where millions of people can communicate with one another. Like all large malls, the Internet has numerous entrances, information centers, levels, concourses, and specialized areas. Box 1.1 shows some of the cyber-places—the virtual gatherings, events, information sites, and services—you can currently explore on the Internet.

1b Connecting to the Internet

Getting on the Internet is not difficult. All you need is a computer, a modem, and browsing software. A **modem** connects a computer to a phone line; a **browser** helps you find places on the Internet. While individual computers may differ in how they are connected to the Internet, nearly all Internet connections provide the same basic services. Your **Internet service provider (ISP)**—perhaps your school's computer center, your telephone or cable company, a local or national commercial service, or a government or nonprofit organization—connects your computer to the Internet.

If you're connecting to the Internet from your home or apartment, enlist the services of an ISP. Your ISP will assign you a **username** (sometimes called an *account name* or a *userid*) and a **password**. Get the name and telephone number of a contact person to call at your ISP in case you have trouble connecting (e.g., if your password no longer works). Keep your ISP account information in a safe place. If you suspect your own computer is the source of your trouble, consult a computer technician.

If you're working with your own Internet connection, you can find help in Internet access guides, such as Adam Engst's *Internet Starter Kit* series for Macintosh and Windows computers. The *ISK* books are available in print from Hayden Books and are also published online at <http://www.mcp.com/hayden/iskm/book.html>, with related software at <ftp://ftp.tidbits.com/pub>. When you've made your Internet connection, go to Chapters 2 and 3 of *Online!* for tips about accessing specific Internet sources.

To learn more about the Internet, its history, how it works, or emerging Internet technologies, visit the following **Web sites**:

Walt Howe, "When Did the Internet Start? A Brief Capsule History"
<http://www.delphi.com/navnet/faq/history.html>
Internet Update
<http://www.itworks.be/EyeonIT/current.html>

Internet Update is a free online magazine, published every Friday, that looks at new developments, products, and trends in the cyberworld.

1c Navigating the Internet's World Wide Web

When you go to the **World Wide Web**, you enter a world of **hypertext** connections linking millions of electronic sites. Your computer communicates with such **Web sites** by following a set of basic rules called **TCP/IP (transmission control protocol/Internet protocol)** that provide a common language usable by all computer operating systems. **Browsers**—software programs that translate your keyboard-and-mouse activities into TCP/IP—find the multimedia information you seek and display it on your screen. When your computer retrieves information for you, it acts as a **client** working with **servers** (other computers).

The earliest Web browsers searched for and retrieved documents containing only text; today's browsers are also able to transmit images, sound, and video. If you connect to the Internet through **direct access** (described in Chapter 2), you can use a *graphic browser* that provides full-color images and easy-to-use menus for navigating the Web, saving and printing documents, and many other options. Popular graphic browsers include Netscape Navigator, Netscape Communicator, and Microsoft Internet Explorer. If you have **indirect access** (described in Chapter 3), you will probably use Lynx, the major surviving *text-only browser*.

Nearly all of the information available on the Web is published in Web pages composed of hypertext. Written in **HTML (hypertext markup language)**, Web pages contain **hypertext links**—usually represented by high-lighted words or pictures—that alert you to the easy availability of more information. The links in a document may point to other portions of the same document, to other documents at the same location, or to any other document anywhere on the Internet. The hypertexts and their links form a three-dimensional electronic "web."

1d Understanding URLs

Every hypertext link contains a **URL (uniform resource locator)** that points to a specific Web site. Most URLs represent the address of a computer file or **directory** (collection of files).

1 Dissecting URLs

Here is how a typical URL looks:

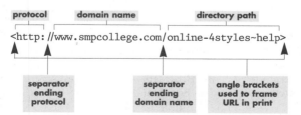

protocol   domain name   directory path

`<http://www.smpcollege.com/online-4styles~help>`

separator ending protocol   separator ending domain name   angle brackets used to frame URL in print

While some Internet humorists would have you believe that the abbreviation **HTTP** means "head to this point," it actually stands for **hypertext transfer protocol**. In a URL, the prefix *http:* represents the **protocol** (kind of link to be made). The two **forward slashes** after the colon show that the link will be to another computer. (URLs use forward slashes, never the backward slashes used in DOS directory paths.) The **domain name** identifies the owner of the Web site (in this case, St. Martin's Press); the last part of the domain name, *.com,* shows that the owner is a commercial entity. A slash separates the domain name from the **directory path**, which is the "address" of the part of the Web site that this particular URL leads to. **Angle brackets** separate the URL from surrounding text.

URLs for World Wide Web sites always begin with *http://*. Other frequently used Internet protocols and their prefixes include **FTP** (*ftp://*), **gopher** (*gopher://*), news (*news://*), **telnet** (*telnet://*), **WAIS** (*wais://*), and the mail protocol *mailto:* (which does not use slashes). URLs for these protocols follow the *http://* pattern but often include other elements such as an **email address** or a **newsgroup** name.

When you click on an onscreen link, your browser uses the associated URL to retrieve the information and display it on your computer. Every browser also includes a **dialog box** where you can enter a URL; pressing the Enter key sends your browser into action. Furthermore, you can use your browser's **bookmark** feature to record the URL and, later, to return quickly to the same page.

Chapter 4 includes more help with finding and using URLs, and the *Online!* Web site offers tricks to try with URLs that don't seem to work.

To learn more about the technical details of URLs, consult the Web document *Names and Addresses, URIs, URLs, URNs, URCs* at <http://www.w3.org/pub/WWW/Addressing/Addressing.html>.

2 Typing URLs

Take care when typing a URL because every letter, symbol, and punctuation mark is significant for computer communication; any extra or missing marks or spaces will prevent you from making a successful link. Always reproduce capitalization accurately. When showing URLs as part of text you're writing, enclose each URL in **angle brackets**—< >—for two reasons:

1. Enclosing a URL in angle brackets tells readers that everything within the brackets is part of the URL (even if the printed text breaks the URL in the middle so that it appears on two lines).
2. Bracketing a URL lets you use punctuation around the URL without introducing ambiguity about whether the punctuation is part of the URL.

The following sentence shows how angle brackets clarify where a URL begins and ends:

▶ For clear answers to questions about grammar, style, and usage, visit the Purdue On-Line Writing Laboratory at <http://owl.english .purdue.edu>; you'll especially enjoy its linked advice on punctuation at <http://owl.english .purdue.edu/files/punctuation.html>.

URLs can be extremely long, running to hundreds of characters. In printed text, a long URL must often be divided. The following rules for breaking URLs are adapted from *Wired Style* (HardWired, 1996), written by the editors of *Wired* magazine:

- *Break a URL after the protocol abbreviation that begins it–http://, gopher://, ftp://;* don't break the abbreviation.
- *Break a URL before a punctuation mark,* moving the punctuation mark to the following line. (The following symbols function as punctuation marks in URLs: tilde ~, hyphen -, underscore _, period or dot ., forward slash /, backslash \, pipe |.)
- *As a last resort, break a URL in the middle of a word,* where you would normally hyphenate the word (but don't hyphenate the break).

Here are examples of acceptable breaks for URLs:

▶   <gopher://
gopher.inform.umd.edu/00/EdRes/ReadingRoom>

▶ <http://lcs.www.media.mit.edu/people/asb /moose-crossing>

▶ <http://www.w3.org/pub/WWW/Address ing/Addressing.html>

Finally, when you enter a URL into your browser's dialog box, remember to type everything *except the angle brackets.*

1e Narrowing a general topic

You can use the Internet to narrow a general topic to a more specific topic you want to research. Suppose you're interested in researching adoption. The Internet is rapidly becoming *the* major clearinghouse for adoption information because it connects people with sources on all aspects of adoption issues and permits quick exchange of information. **Surfing** Internet discussions of child adoption, you'll find a wide range of information, from scholarly expertise to personal pleas for help. One of the greatest achievements of the Internet is that it lets everyone's electronic voice be heard.

A preliminary Internet search on child adoption reveals many possible subtopics:

Searching for one's biological parents or children

Searching for prospective adoptive parents or children

Learning how to evaluate the health of available adoptees

Finding sources of support for adoptive families

Reading and analyzing stories about adoption

Working to improve adoption law

Each item on this list represents vast amounts of electronically published materials available in many forms. The main difficulty is not so much knowing where to begin — you could just go to the library and look up *adoption* — but knowing how to narrow your focus quickly, to browse through sources comprehensively yet efficiently. Although some very important resources such as legal databases and hospital birth records are not yet Internet-connected and must be accessed in more traditional ways, many adoption organizations provide Internet help in using such services. Internet tools for surveying and narrowing a topic are described in 1g-1.

1f Researching a specific topic

Sometimes you'll start your research with a fairly specific topic in mind. Suppose you want to know more about Charlotte Perkins Gilman's "The Yellow Wallpaper," a short story published in 1892 that recounts a woman's descent into depression and (perhaps) insanity as she struggles to express herself within her husband's agonizing restrictions. Because of its feminist elements and its powerful description of depression, the story appears regularly on reading lists for courses in literature, psychology, and women's studies. If you do an Internet text search for the **keywords** *yellow wallpaper*, you'll retrieve hundreds of **hits** (items matching your request), including many Web pages for classes where the story is being discussed. Among these pages is *The* Yellow Wallpaper *Site* at <http://www.cwrl.utexas.edu /~daniel/amlit/wallpaper/wallpaper .html>, created to accompany an American literature course and maintained as an ongoing Web project. Through this page you can read an online edition of the story, find historical details about the author and the story's publication, read critics' comments and students' essays, select related Internet links, and even contribute to the ongoing discussion. If you leave a comment or ask a question, perhaps about the story's puzzling ending, your message automatically appears within the forum, and others can then reply to you the same way.

To see what other literary works are being explored similarly, visit the *American Literature Survey Site* at <http://www.cwrl.utexas.edu/~daniel/amlit/amlit .htm> or search the Internet for the phrase *interactive texts*. For example, the *Shakespeare Discussion Area* at <http://the-tech.mit.edu/Shakespeare/cgi-bin /commentary/get/main.html> houses evolving commentary on all of Shakespeare's works, with links to the complete texts.

1g-2 describes Internet tools for researching a specific topic.

1g   Searching with Internet tools

You can use many different programs to search for information. Selecting the most efficient **search tool** for a particular topic usually means choosing between two kinds of tools: those providing **subject directories** and those listing **text indexes**.

Subject directories work like telephone book yellow pages, listing Web sites by predetermined categories. You select a category by clicking the headings on the directory's homepage, or use the directory's search func-

> **Box 1.2**
> **Some popular subject-directory search tools**
>
> **The Argus Clearinghouse** <http://www.clearinghouse.net>
> **Inter-Links** <http://www.nova.edu/Inter-Links>
> **The Internet Public Library** <http://www.ipl.org>
> **The Internet Services List** <http://www.spectracom
> .com/islist>
> **Library of Congress World Wide Web Home Page**
> <http://lcweb.loc.gov>
> **The WWW Virtual Library** <http://www.w3.org/vl>
> **Yahoo!** <http://www.yahoo.com>

tion to find categories that contain the term you're interested in. Then the directory shows you any relevant subcategories and sites. When you click on a site's link, you leave the directory's menus and visit that page. You can then return to the directory's page with your browser's Back button.

Text indexes let you scan documents for specific terms. The indexing service uses robot programs that periodically comb through the Internet, recording each occurrence of every word or phrase found. When you enter a search term, the index returns a list of sites that contained your term when the robot last cataloged them. Search results differ from one index to another, mostly because of varying scope and frequency of cataloging.

When you want to see what the Internet offers about a broad topic, use a subject directory; when you want to see which Internet sites contain a particular word or phrase, use a text index.

1 Subject directories

Suppose you know the broad topic you want to research, but you haven't yet chosen a narrower subtopic to focus on. For example, you might be interested in child adoption but not know what subtopics were available for exploration. To find out, you could use one or more of the search tools listed in Box 1.2. All these tools index the World Wide Web's contents by subject category and offer the results in a subject directory. This section describes some of the most useful subject-directory search tools.

Yahoo!
<http://www.yahoo.com>

Yahoo! is one of the most popular subject-directory search tools. Its **homepage**, shown in Figure 1.2, offers links to more than a dozen major categories such as Arts and Humanities, Education, Entertainment, Health, Recreation and Sports, Reference, and Society and Culture. After opening a category, you keep choosing from successive menus until you reach a list of Web sites you may want to visit. Or, using the dialog box on the Yahoo! main screen, you can retrieve Yahoo! categories containing specific keywords, or individual sites whose titles or short descriptions contain your keywords. The list of **hits** for a Yahoo! search also offers links to other search tools.

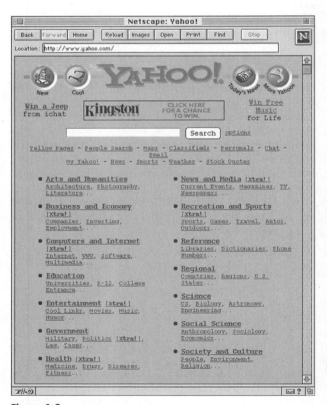

Figure 1.2
The homepage for Yahoo!
<http://www.yahoo.com>

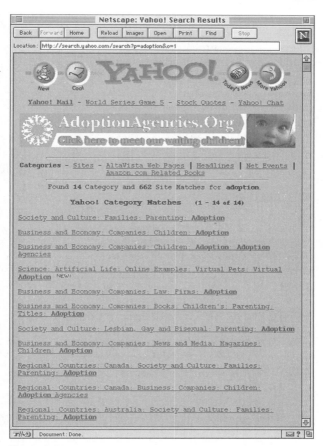

Figure 1.3
A search results screen from Yahoo!

If you typed the word *adoption* into the Yahoo! dialog box, you would get a list much like that in Figure 1.3. If you clicked on Society and Culture: Families: Parenting: Adoption, you would get a menu that included Organizations. This hotlink would take you to a list of links to the resources of groups such as Adoptees in Search at <http://members.aol.com/aisdenver/adoption .htm>, the National Adoption Center at <http://www .nac.adopt.org/nac/nac.html>, and the Surrogate Mothers Network (at <http://www.phoenix.net/~townhall /surrogat/surrogat.html>. The Yahoo! menu for adoption organizations probably doesn't include all Internet-connected adoption organizations, because the database doesn't (yet) include every document available on the Internet, and because its index may place a particular agency's document in another category.

The Argus Clearinghouse
<http://www.clearinghouse.net>

The Clearinghouse specializes in monitoring a large collection of **subject guides**, or **webliographies**. From the homepage, shown in Figure 1.4, you can select subjects

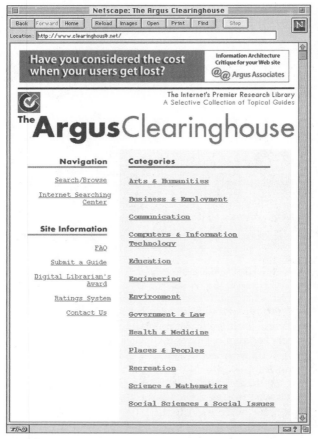

Figure 1.4
The homepage of The Argus Clearinghouse
<http://www.clearinghouse.net>

Figure 1.5
A search results screen from The Argus Clearinghouse

by category or search for keywords. By searching for the
term *adoption,* for example, you would discover that the
Clearinghouse has at least three recommended guides.
(See Figure 1.5.) The links within each guide take you to
individual adoption-related sites.

What distinguishes the Clearinghouse from other
subject directories is its guide rating system. Each subject guide is rated for its detailed descriptions of the listed sites. Although the Clearinghouse rating does not
apply to individual Web pages listed in a guide, the
comments in a Clearinghouse-approved guide are likely
to be worthwhile. See 4c-7 for further information about
these ratings.

Inter-Links
<http://www.nova.edu/Inter-Links>

The Inter-Links homepage offers broad categories such
as Topical Resources, News and Weather, and Reference
Shelf. Clicking on these categories takes you to all the
basic Internet search tools as well as onscreen help. The

Web site's self-description "About Inter-Links" explains that "Care is taken to provide links to resources that are informative, stable (i.e., regularly accessible), primarily free and with a minimum of advertising, and likely to appeal to a wide range of people."

The Internet Public Library
<http://www.ipl.org>

The homepage of the Internet Public Library (IPL) recalls the lobby of a real library, with links to areas such as Reference, Teen, and Adult. According to the IPL's "Mission Statement," "The Internet is a mess. Since nobody runs it, that's no surprise." The librarians propose to clean up the "mess," using their organizing skills to help people find and use information that is interesting and worthwhile. A special feature is the IPL Reference Center at <http://www.ipl.org /ref>. At this site, librarians will answer your questions by email.

Other subject-directory search tools At The Internet Services List, The WWW Virtual Library, and the Library of Congress World Wide Web Home Page, you'll find guides to Web resources for hundreds of subject areas. Typical subject guides include lists of Web, gopher, telnet, and FTP sites and listservs and newsgroups. The Internet Services List at <http://www.spectracom.com /islist> uses a relatively simple hierarchy to lead to useful sources you might not find through search tools focusing only on Web documents. The WWW Virtual Library, described by the magazine *Publishers Weekly* as "the granddaddy of sites on the Internet," has links arranged according to the topics used by the Library of Congress. You'll find the Library at <http://www.w3 .org/vl>. To examine one of the most extensive lists of Internet subject directories, visit the Library of Congress World Wide Web Home Page at <http://lcweb.loc.gov>, which has exceptionally useful links to search tools that provide information on all Internet sources.

2 Text indexes

If you already know which aspect of a topic you want to investigate, you can use a search tool that scans the text of every document within its text index for the keywords you specify and prepares a results menu with links to documents containing the keywords. If you used a text-indexing tool to search for material about a broad topic, you might get an unmanageably long list of hits. For example, a search for the keyword *adoption* in 1997 with one text index produced more than 120,000 hits. Narrowing the search to *transracial adoption* reduced the number of indexed sites to fewer than 150.

This section describes some of the most useful text-indexing search tools. (For more advice on searching with such tools, see 4b-2 and 4b-3.)

AltaVista
<http://altavista.digital.com>

One of the most comprehensive Internet search tools, AltaVista indexes the full text of more than 30 million Web pages and several million newsgroup messages. You can perform a "Simple" search using the dialog box on the opening screen, or select an "Advanced" search screen that lets you specify more precise relationships among keywords and request that hits containing certain terms be listed first. You can also specify how much detail the list of hits should include. AltaVista generally gives more extensive results than other search tools, but you may have to look through many menus to find the most relevant items.

Figure 1.6 (on page 30) shows the first few hits resulting from an AltaVista search for the term *transracial adoption* in September 1997. The words, when typed in the dialog box, were enclosed in quotation marks so the search engine would treat them as a phrase. (Had we not used quotation marks, the results would have included all sites containing both words, regardless of their order or proximity. You can use this quotation-mark strategy whenever a search for a multiple-word term returns too many hits.) AltaVista lists the results in sets of ten links per page, with onscreen buttons to click from one set to another.

More complex search strategies can be used with AltaVista's "advanced" search screen, easily reached from the homepage. The Advanced Search dialog box lets you specify relationships between your search terms with the words AND, OR, NOT, and NEAR. For example, to find information about transracial adoptions in Texas, you might use an Advanced Search for the

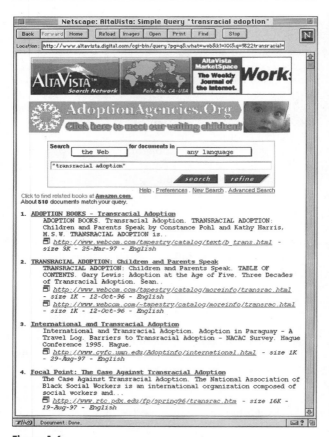

Figure 1.6
Some results of an AltaVista search
<http://altavista.digital.com>

expression *"transracial adoption" NEAR Texas*. For more tips on search strategies, see the Help screens linked to AltaVista's search pages.

Open Text
<http://www.opentext.com>

Open Text gives you many ways to control the use of search terms—for example, by restricting the search for a particular term to a document's title or text. This method adds precision to the search, and the ranked results may provide more convenient access to important sources than AltaVista does, but the relatively small number of documents indexed by Open Text (about 2 million pages) means that you're likely to miss many relevant sources.

Lycos
<http://www.lycos.com>

Lycos indexes about 20 million Web documents. The main search page has a dialog box much like AltaVista's, while the custom search page lets you decide whether the match should be "loose," "fair," "good," "close," or "strong." These adjectives successively reduce the number of hits reported, but Lycos doesn't explain what the adjectives mean (e.g., how close a "close" match really is). You can also specify how many of your terms must be matched at once (e.g., "match 3 terms" or "match 4 terms") and how detailed the results must be. Documents are ranked according to how many of your search terms they contain.

Other text-index search tools Box 1.3 lists URLs for many helpful search tools. Netscape's Net Search offers links to many other tools. For novelty, you might consider the All-In-One Search Page, which allows direct searching with more than 100 search tools, or Savvy

---

Box 1.3
Some popular text-indexing search tools

All-in-One Search Page <http://www.albany.net/allinone>
AltaVista <http://altavista.digital.com>
Excite <http://excite.com>
Inference Find <http://www.inference.com/ifind>
Infoseek Guide <http://guide.infoseek.com>
Lycos <http://www.lycos.com>
Magellan <http://www.mckinley.com>
Metacrawler <http://www.metacrawler.com>
Net Search <http://home.netscape.com/escapes/search/index.html>
Open Text <http://www.opentext.com>
Savvy Search <http://www.savvysearch.com>
Search.com <http://www.search.com>
WebCrawler <http://www.webcrawler.com>

Search, which requests searches from several tools at the same time. Inference Find, Metacrawler, and Search.com exemplify **metaengines**, tools that analyze and sort results from several searches. Subject-specific search tools—such as Hippias, a philosophy index at <http://hippias.evansville.edu>—are proliferating too rapidly to be included in Box 1.3, but you can find them easily from a subject directory such as Yahoo!

3 More about search tools

New Internet search tools appear almost every month, and existing search tools are continually being improved. As you encounter new or revised tools, be sure to check their Help documents for the latest developments and search hints. For up-to-date comparisons of search tools, consult the links within the Yahoo! menu "Comparing Search Engines" at <http://www .yahoo.com/Computers_and_Internet/Internet/World _Wide_Web/Searching_the_Web>. A thorough comparison of some common search strategies, "Great Web Searching: Tricks of the Trade" by Peggy Zorn, Mary Emanoil, Lucy Marshall, and Mary Panek, is available in print (*Online*, May/June 1996, 14–28) and at <http:// www.onlineinc.com/onlinemag/MayOL/zorn5.html>.

Try it yourself!

1. Use your Web browser to visit the site for this book at <http://www.smpcollege.com/online-4styles~help>. (See 1d-2 if you need help using a URL with your browser.) Be sure to bookmark this site immediately. (See 2a if you need help with bookmarks.)

2. Visit a subject directory (see 1g-1) and locate a subject guide for a topic that interests you.

3. Look at several text indexes (see 1g-2) and compare the results you get when you use them to search for the same term. Can you find the help pages for each service?

CHAPTER TWO

Connecting to the Internet by Direct Access

You can visit the Internet through direct or indirect access. You have direct access to the Internet if your personal computer (or the computer terminal you're using) has all the software you need to visit the Internet. You may have to connect to a network or dial into another system by a direct-access protocol (e.g., TCP/IP, PPP, SLIP, or CSLIP), but after that you can use graphic browsers such as Netscape Navigator, Netscape Communicator, Microsoft Internet Explorer, and NCSA Mosaic just as you use other programs on your computer. Web pages appearing on your screen will present text, graphics, sound, animation, and video. (Your browser may require additional pieces of software, commonly called plug-ins, to display some of these special effects; the browser will alert you to the need for such software and even lead you through the process of

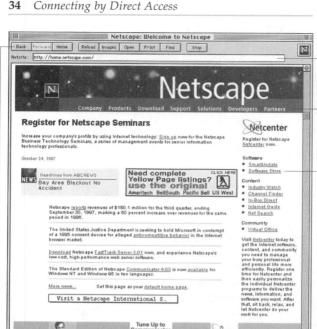

Navigation buttons   Status line   Button for mail   Screen scroll bar

Links to select   Location box

Figure 2.1
A screen in Netscape Navigator
<http://guide.netscape.com/guide>

downloading and installing it.) Figures 2.1 and 2.2 show the basic onscreen features of two popular browsers.

Direct access lets you visit Web sources by typing in a source's **URL** or by using your mouse to navigate through **hyperlinks** on your screen. This chapter gives guidelines for accessing nine types of Internet sources.

2a   Direct access to the World Wide Web

The World Wide Web—often called the Web—is a network of **hypertext** documents. (See 1c for a fuller description of the Web.) Each document has an "address" called a **URL (uniform resource locator)**. (See 1d.) Web page URLs always begin with the **HTTP** protocol, which appears in URLs as *http://*. For accessing URLs, most graphic browsers provide a **dialog box** — which might be labeled "Location" or "Go To" or "Netsite" — with space for typing in a full HTTP address. To reach a Web site whose URL you know, type the URL into the box. (If you're working from within another text that contains the URL you want to reach, use your computer's Copy and Paste commands to insert the URL into the box.)

For example, to reach the **Web site** of Project Gutenberg, which is making classic texts available in electronic format, you would type:

▶ http://www.promo.net/pg

Figure 2.3 (on page 36) shows the Project Gutenberg **homepage**. With many browsers you don't have to type *http://* at the beginning of a URL; the browser automatically inserts the prefix for you.

A key feature of browser navigation is the use of **bookmarks** or **favorites**, a list of sites you decide you want to visit again. Here's how to compile a **bookmark list**: while visiting a site, you use a menu option or

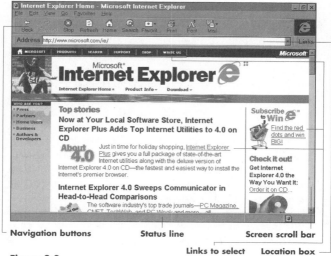

Navigation buttons   **Status line**   **Screen scroll bar**

Links to select   **Location box**

Figure 2.2
A screen in Internet Explorer
<http://home.microsoft.com>

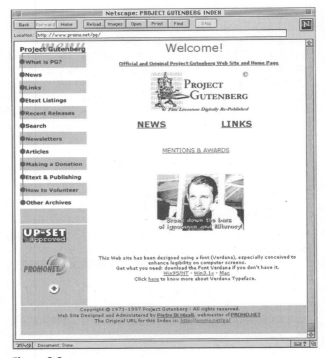

Figure 2.3
The Project Gutenberg homepage
<http://www.promo.net/pg>

screen button to save a bookmark, which stores the
address and lets you return quickly to the site later by
selecting its entry from your bookmark list. If you share
a computer with other users, you can save your bookmarks to a file, store the file on a floppy disk, and later
import it to the browser again.

When you subscribe with an **Internet service
provider**, you usually receive an installation software
package that includes one of the popular browsers. Most
ISPs let you use whatever browser you prefer; notable
exceptions include America Online and CompuServe,
whose communication programs are compatible only
with their own browsers. To obtain up-to-date browser
software, visit the company's homepage and follow the
downloading instructions. Read the license agreement
carefully to see whether you must pay for the software.

Here are the homepages of two popular browsers:

Microsoft Internet Explorer
<http://www.microsoft.com>

Netscape Communicator and Netscape Navigator
<http://www.netscape.com>

2b Direct access to email

Email (electronic mail) works like the postal system (only much faster!), transmitting messages to individuals and groups over computer networks. While you'll find many personal uses for email, in your research you will most likely use it for the following:

- Requesting information about authors and sources
- Using email links in Web documents
- Using **listservs**

Graphic browsers include all normal mail-handling functions. For example, with Netscape Navigator you can select the Netscape Mail window, then read or send messages. Mail-only programs such as Eudora offer specialized ways to organize your mail. Versions of Eudora are available at no cost for Macintosh and Windows users at <ftp://ftp.qualcomm.com/eudora /eudoralight>.

Sending an email message usually involves little more than clicking a New Message button or menu item; typing the recipient's address, a **subject line**, and your text; and clicking a Send button. Your name and email

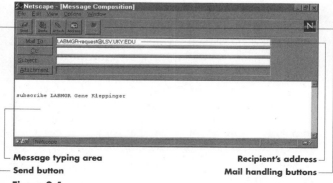

Message typing area   Recipient's address
Send button   Mail handling buttons

Figure 2.4
Sending email in Netscape Navigator

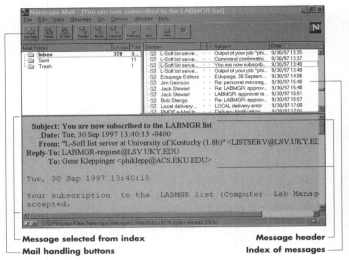

Message selected from index

Mail handling buttons

Message header

Index of messages

Figure 2.5
Reading email in Netscape Navigator

address are automatically included in the message
header. To read an incoming message, you click an entry
in a list and see the message in its own window. Figures
2.4 and 2.5 show typical email sending and reading
screens.

Most email programs enable you to use the following
special functions:

CC: — A line in the header that lets you send a "carbon
copy" of your message to a third party

Attachments — Files such as word-processed documents, graphics, or spreadsheets that you want to
include with your message

Hypertext links — URLs you type into your message
that appear on your recipient's screen as active links,
ready to be followed

Signature file — Lines of text (and/or a graphic) that
are automatically added to the end of every message
you send (for example, you might include your name,
your title, your school's or company's name, your
address, and any other contact information)

Address book — A way of storing your collection of
email addresses

See 9c for more information about using email.

2c Direct access to Web discussion forums

Web discussion forums are sites designed to facilitate online debate and information exchange. Their structure incorporates features of several other kinds of Internet sources:

- Like most Web pages, these sites have hypertext links and graphics.

- Like email (see 2b), the messages you can read have a personal tone, usually including names and email addresses.

- As in newsgroups (see 2e), the discussion follows threads that are displayed onscreen as a series of messages and replies.

In **HyperNews**, a popular Web discussion program, each **article** an ordinary-looking *http*: URL that lets you retrieve the article as you would any other Web page (i.e., by clicking on an onscreen link or typing into a dialog box). (To see how this works, look at Figures 2.6 and 2.7 or visit the HyperNews homepage at <http://www.hypernews.org>.) When integrated into a Web page's design, the HyperNews format preserves **threads** (series of articles about a particular topic) and lets you contribute responses that immediately appear as new articles under the relevant thread heading. In short,

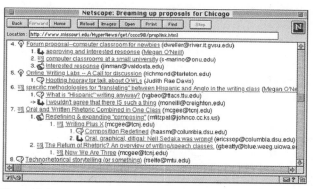

Figure 2.6
Part of the hierarchy of HyperNews responses for
<http://www.missouri.edu/HyperNews/get/cccc98/proplink.html>

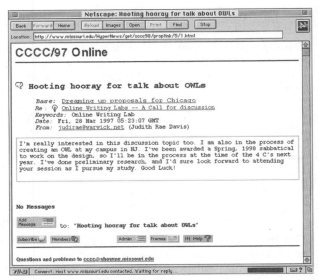

Figure 2.7
One of the HyperNews messages listed in Figure 2.6

HyperNews gives you access both to an ongoing conversation and to the conversation's history.

If you use a graphic browser, you shouldn't need any
additional software to access discussion forums.

2d   Direct access to listservs

Listservs are ongoing email discussions about technical
or nontechnical issues, covering the spectrum from abo-
riginal languages to zoology. Messages are typically
announcements, questions, position statements, or
replies and are distributed to the personal email boxes of
all of the listserv's members.

In order to start receiving a particular listserv's
postings, you must subscribe to the listserv from your
own email account. *Important: Never send a listserv subscription request to the list's own address.* Listservs have a
separate address for handling subscriptions, and subscribers understandably become annoyed when they
must sort out subscription requests from useful messages. As you uncover interesting listservs, pay careful

attention to the *separate addresses for subscribing to a list and for sending messages to the list.*

For example, to subscribe to the Macintosh News and Information list, you would send the message *subscribe MAC-L* [your name] to <listserv@yalevm.cis.yale.edu>. To send messages to the list members, you would use the address <mac-l@yalevm.cis.yale.edu>. Lists that work through programs besides the trademarked LIST-SERV software, such as ListProc and Majordomo, have slightly different subscription procedures. You can find information about listservs in most **subject directories** or in listserv indexes such as those listed on the Inter-Links "Email Discussion Groups" page at <http://www .nova.edu/Inter-Links/listserv.html>.

Listservs include *open lists* (to which anyone may subscribe and **post** messages), *moderated lists* (where a human **moderator** reviews messages before they go to subscribers), and *closed lists* (where you must request permission or explain your goals before being permitted to join). Discussions may range from technical analyses of narrow topics to friendly brainstorming. After subscribing to a listserv, observe the message traffic for a few days (or review the list's **archives**) to get a feel for the list's "personality" before contributing your own message. With most unmoderated lists, *anything* you send to the list address is forwarded immediately to every subscriber.

See 9d for more on using listservs.

2e Direct access to newsgroups

The **Usenet** network provides access to many thousands of electronic discusssion groups called **newsgroups**. Unlike listserv messages (see 2d), which are delivered to your private email box, Usenet messages are collected on a system called a *news server,* where anyone with access to Usenet can retrieve them.

Here is a typical newsgroup name:

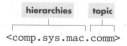

The first part of the name specifies the Usenet *hierarchy* (category) to which the group belongs—in this case, *comp.* for computer-related topics. A **dot** separates the hierarchy from the rest of the name, which specifies the newsgroup's topic through successively narrower sub-hierarchies—in this case, communications programs for Macintosh computer systems.

There are hundreds of Usenet hierarchies. Major ones besides *comp.* include *news.* for Usenet information, *rec.* for recreational activities and hobbies, *sci.* for scientific topics, *soc.* for social, political, and religious subjects, *talk.* for opinion, and *misc.* and *alt.* for topics that don't fit elsewhere.

Graphic browsers will accept URLs containing the *news:* **protocol**, as in <news:alt.adoption>, provided your browser's Options or Preferences screens specify a news server. (If you need to specify your news server, try the same address as your mail server or ask your system staff or **Internet service provider** for help.) Some browsers provide a separate window with Usenet-oriented functions. The browser retrieves and displays the messages you seek; it may also let you post your own messages.

If you can't use your browser to access news-groups, you may be able to use a *newsreader* program; try News Xpress for Windows at <ftp:// ftp.tidbits .com/pub/tiskwin/nx10b2.zip> or NewsWatcher for Macintosh at <ftp://ftp.tidbits.com/pub/tidbits/tisk /tcp/newswatcher-216.hqx>, or ask a computer expert for help.

For advice on participating in newsgroups, see 9e.

2f Direct access to real-time communication

Real-time communication allows two or more people to participate in an ongoing online conversation, whether they are socializing, playing games, or forming a "virtual community" for learning. The simplest form of real-time communication, a program called Talk, lets two people chat online, displaying their messages on the halves of a divided screen. This "synchronous" communication differs from **asynchronous** (delayed) **communication** such as email because each person's message appears onscreen as fast as it is being typed.

IRC (Internet relay chat), the online equivalent of CB radio and telephone conferencing, is organized into channels where groups of people "gather" to chat. You

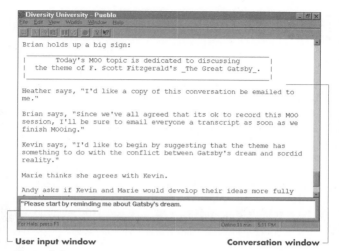

Brian holds up a big sign:

> Today's MOO topic is dedicated to discussing
> the theme of F. Scott Fitzgerald's _The Great Gatsby_.

Heather says, "I'd like a copy of this conversation be emailed to me."

Brian says, "Since we've all agreed that its ok to record this MOO session, I'll be sure to email everyone a transcript as soon as we finish MOOing."

Kevin says, "I'd like to begin by suggesting that the theme has something to do with the conflict between Gatsby's dream and sordid reality."

Marie thinks she agrees with Kevin.

Andy asks if Kevin and Marie would develop their ideas more fully

"Please start by reminding me about Gatsby's dream.

User input window   **Conversation window**

Figure 2.8
A fragment of conversation at Diversity University MOO
<telnet://moo.du.org:8888>

can use IRC by telnetting to a public-access client's address or by finding a chat zone on the Web.

Among the most potent expressions of Internet inter-activity are **MUDs** and **MOOs**, which provide electronic "spaces" where people can "meet." **MUD** stands for **multi-user domain**. If a MUD is *object-oriented* (meaning that you can type commands to create and manipulate **virtual** objects—tables, pets, or anything imaginable), it's called a **MOO (multi-user domain, object-oriented)**. These forms of virtual reality on the Internet are frequently used for online classes and conferences. Right now almost all MUD and MOO communication is limited to text (see Figure 2.8), although some sites are adding a graphic window to integrate pictures or video with the typed conversation.

The URL for a MUD or MOO site begins with the *telnet://* protocol and usually ends with a port number. Here's the URL for Diversity University MOO:

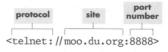

protocol   **site**   **port number**
<telnet: //moo.du.org:8888>

Your browser can open such a URL as long as it can find a **telnet** program (see 2g), but there are drawbacks to telnetting to a MUD or MOO through your browser: your screen shows all messages as a continuous flow, and your own typing sometimes gets interrupted by others' messages, with very confusing results. If you must use this method, get advice from Nick Carbone's document "Telnet Help Sheet for MOOing" at <http://www.daedalus.com/net/telnet.html>.

For frequent MUD or MOO exploration, you may want to use a **client** program that gives you better control over what you type and what you see onscreen. Many client programs are available for Macintosh, Unix, and Windows systems; for reviews, see Jennifer Smith's "Frequently Asked/Answered Questions" at <http://www.c2-tech.com/~jds/mudfaqs.html>. The *Online!* Web site offers links to download several MUD/MOO clients. Web pages that give information about basic MUD/MOO commands and describe various sites include Jeffrey Galin's "MOO Central" at <http://www.pitt.edu/~jrgst7/MOOcentral.html>, Traci Gardner's "MOO Teacher's Tip Sheet" at <http://www.daedalus.com/net/MOOTIPS.html>, and Lydia Leong's "The MUD Resource Collection" at http://www.godlike.com/muds>.

Section 9f gives advice on participating in real-time communication.

2g Direct access to telnet

Telnet is an Internet protocol that lets you log onto another computer from your computer. When you type a URL such as

into your browser's window, the browser connects to the site using a separate telnet program on your system. If you don't already have a telnet program, you can get one directly from the Internet via **FTP** (at no cost) through the *Online!* Web site or from <ftp://ftp.tidbits.com>.

Web pages occasionally include telnet links, with onscreen instructions for their use. Knowing how to use telnet is also important when you want to connect through the Internet to run programs on a computer other than the one you're seated at (e.g., to use your campus account while you're away from school).

A telnet session opens in a new window on your screen. This window has no graphics and may show a blinking cursor awaiting your keyboard command. (Telnet can't send instructions from your computer's mouse to the computer you're trying to reach, although you may be able to use your mouse with your own software to highlight text on the screen in order to save it, print it, or copy it for use in your wordprocessor.) Once you're connected, watch for a message about an *escape character;* knowing the character will make it easy to end the connection when you're finished. As the session begins, you may get further instructions (e.g., "login as *visitor* and use password *guest*").

To end a telnet session, type the other computer system's escape command. If no command is listed, try *exit* or *quit* or press ^] or ^C (where ^ means that you hold down the Control key).

2h Direct access to FTP

FTP (file transfer protocol) transports files between computers on the Internet. Here's a typical FTP site URL:

You can type the URL command into your browser's dialog box. If you have only a site name, such as <ftp .tidbits.com>, construct a usable URL with the *ftp://* prefix: <ftp://ftp.tidbits.com>. If your browser responds "invalid URL" when you specify a site name, try adding a **forward slash** at the end of the URL: thus, <ftp:// wuarchive.wustl.edu> becomes <ftp://wuarchive.wustl .edu/>.

The most common use for FTP is downloading software such as updates or **plug-ins** for your existing programs and for new programs you want to try. Computer hardware manufacturers often place improved software for their devices on their Web sites for FTP delivery to their customers.

If you get a "login incorrect" message after attempting an FTP connection through your browser, the other computer did not accept your browser's automatic method for anonymous identification. (Most FTP **servers** expect your computer to use *anonymous* as your **username** and your email address as your **password**.) Consider using a separate FTP program (see the end of this section for advice), or try typing the expected identification as a URL in your browser's **dialog box**, according to the following special pattern:

▶ ftp://anonymous:username%40system.dom@ftphost
  name.dom

The symbols %40 in the pattern represent the @ sign in your email address. (The @ sign itself has a different meaning when it appears in a URL.)

Although browsers are designed to handle FTP, you may have trouble in particular situations. One frequent problem with FTP arises when files in *binary* format are mistakenly transferred as *text* files, or vice versa. Binary files, such as programs or program archives, images, and formatted files from wordprocessors and spreadsheets, transfer more slowly than text files. Efficient file transfer depends on knowing the proper format for each file. The FTP process itself can't determine which kind of data a particular file contains; instead, it predicts which format to use from the *extension* (final element) in the file's name, such as *zip*, *txt*, or *html*. Currently, graphic browsers don't let you override these predictions, and so the transfer of a file with an inappropriate or unusual extension may fail or may make the file useless to you. If you have trouble using FTP through your usual browser, consider getting a separate program such as Fetch (for Macintosh) or WS_FTP (for Windows) for FTP. You can find Fetch at <ftp://ftp.tidbits.com/pub/tidbits/tisk/tcp/fetch-303.hqx> and WS_FTP at <ftp://ftp.tidbits.com/pub/tiskwin/ws_ftp.zip>.

For more information about using FTP, including detailed instructions for saving various kinds of files, see the document "World Wide Web: Telnet, Gopher and FTP" at <http://www.hsl.unc.edu/HSL/es/ntgftp.htm>.

2i   Direct access to gopher

Gopher, a program for accessing Internet information through menus arranged in hierarchies, will "go for" the information you seek and will display it on your screen.

Gopher URLs look very much like HTTP and FTP addresses but usually contain a crucial one- or two-digit number that specifies the *type* of resource being selected, rather than just naming a file directory. For example, in the imaginary URL

▶ `<gopher: //domain.name.edu/7data/findit>`

the 7 signals a request to use the *findit* search within the *data* directory. Gopher selection pathways often involve characters, especially spaces, that are not allowed in standard URLs and so must be translated with special symbols, resulting in unwieldy strings like <gopher:// gopher.tc.umn.edu/00/Information%20About%20 Gopher/about%09%09%2B>.

For URLs that begin with the *gopher:* protocol, use your regular Web browser. With a very complicated URL, you may find it useful to reach the "root" gopher by typing only the protocol and full server name (in this case, <gopher://gopher.tc.umn.edu>). When you reach the gopher site, use the menus to find the document by deciphering the correct screen selections from the remainder of the URL.

The fundamental search tool for gopher documents, **Veronica**, can be accessed through Web search programs such as Yahoo! and through the Veronica gateway at <http://www.scs.unr.edu/veronica.html>. Although some Web search results include gopher sources, the indexing of gopher sites is not complete, and you may find a separate Veronica search very helpful.

If you're not satisfied with your Web browser's handling of gopher sources, consider using a separate program such as WSGopher for Windows at <gopher:// boombox.micro.umn.edu/59/gopher/Windows /wsg-12> or TurboGopher for Macintosh at <ftp:// boombox.micro.umn.edu/pub/gopher/Macintosh-TurboGopher>.

CHAPTER THREE

Connecting to the Internet by Indirect Access

You can visit the **Internet** through **indirect** or **direct access**. You have **indirect access** (sometimes called *shell access*) if you use a personal computer or networked terminal to log onto another computer (sometimes called a *local host*) and run programs on that computer. You start the connection by using communication software such as HyperTerminal, Kermit, ProComm, QModem, or ZTerm to dial your **modem**. The local host then prompts you to enter your **username** and **password**. During your session, you type commands at a prompt (such as a \$ sign, a % sign, or a system name) or make selections from an onscreen menu. Your menu choices typically include Mail, Pine, Lynx, **FTP**, **gopher**, and **telnet** (and perhaps **WWW**, for **World Wide Web**). Your account entitles you to use a specific amount of disk space (often called your *quota*) for storing your own files at the other computer. The main limitation of indirect access is that it doesn't provide a *graphic interface,* which means that although you can access the text of Web documents, you can't see or use any graphics they may include.

Although indirect accounts don't connect you to the graphics and sound available on the Web, they do have some advantages. First, they're usually free (since they tend to be provided by colleges, universities, and libraries). Furthermore, while graphic **browsers** such as

49

Microsoft Internet Explorer and Netscape Navigator let you see the exciting visual displays that often accompany information, many researchers prefer to use text-only browsers such as Lynx, which retrieve information more quickly, bypassing the slowdown of **downloading** graphics. Even some researchers who do have direct access turn off their browser's ability to retrieve images so that they can gather Internet information more efficiently and print it (or copy it into other documents) more quickly.

Most software for indirect access is built to use *vt100 terminal emulation,* meaning that the software expects to receive commands typed at a terminal keyboard. Find the vt100 setting on your communication program's menu and use it. If you have trouble connecting, get help from your system staff or consider changing your communication software.

This chapter explains how to reach the World Wide Web and other Internet sources through indirect access. The *Online!* Web site offers more details about these topics.

3a Indirect access to the World Wide Web

The **World Wide Web** — often called the Web — is a network of **hypertext** documents. (See 1c for a fuller description of the Web.) Each document has an "address" called a **URL (uniform resource locator)**. (See 1d.) Web-page URLs always begin with the **HTTP** protocol, which appears in URLs as *http://*. (Many Web sites are publicized without the protocol — for example, a television commercial might advertise <www.mci.com> instead of <http://www.mci.com>. When typing a URL into a text browser, remember to add the *http://* prefix.)

Indirect access to the World Wide Web lets you retrieve all the *text* information at any given Web site. If you have indirect access, your browser is probably Lynx. To access Lynx, type *lynx* at your system prompt, or select Lynx from your menu. The first time you use Lynx, go to the Options screen (press o) to name your **bookmark list** and record your **email address**, and then save your changes (press >).

What Lynx displays as it starts depends on settings in the files that control your account. If your system personnel have not designated a specific starting point,

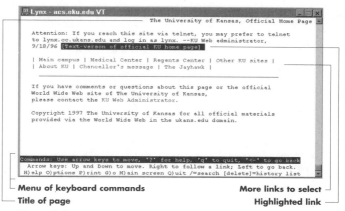

Menu of keyboard commands   More links to select

Title of page   Highlighted link

Figure 3.1
The University of Kansas homepage, viewed with Lynx
<http://lynx.cc.ukans.edu>

you'll see a page about Lynx from the University of
Kansas. (See Figure 3.1.)

When working with Lynx, you use keyboard commands, not mouse movements, to control its operations.
For example, when you are using **hyperlinks**, which
appear as highlighted text on your screen, you press the
Down Arrow key to select the next available link and the
Right Arrow key to retrieve the information from that
link. Box 3.1 gives directions for using Lynx to connect
to the *Online!* Web site, which offers more help with
using Lynx as your browser. For more information
about Lynx, see "Extremely Lynx" at <http://www.crl
.com/~subir/lynx.html>.

Box 3.1
Accessing the *Online!* Web site with Lynx

1. Start Lynx.

2. Press *g*; at the bottom of the screen you will see "Go to URL:".

3. Type *http://www.smpcollege.com/online-4styles~help* and
   press Enter; you will see the *Online!* homepage.

4. Press *a* and then *d* to add a bookmark for this site. (If you
   receive an error message that you have no bookmark file, go
   to the Options screen by pressing *o*.)

5. Now, whenever you are using Lynx, you can go to the *Online!*
   site by pressing *v* and selecting the appropriate link.

3b Indirect access to other Internet sources

The range of Internet sources available to you through indirect access depends on the software installed on the computer system you're using. Besides Lynx, you probably have the following:

- An **email** program such as Mail, Pine, or Elm for access to personal email (see 2b) and **listservs** (see 2d)
- A **newsreader** program such as TRN, NN, or News for access to **newsgroups** (see 2e)
- **Telnet**, a program for connecting to other systems for special services such as **real-time communication** (see 2f and 2g)
- **FTP**, the standard program for moving files from one system to another (see 2h)
- **Gopher**, a program for accessing Internet information through menus arranged in hierarchies (see 2i)

Detailed directions for using these indirect access programs are available on the *Online!* Web site, which you can reach through Lynx. (See Box 3.1 on page 51.)

CHAPTER FOUR

Choosing and Evaluating Internet Sources

While **Internet** sources can be informative and valuable, they should generally complement information from traditional print sources, not replace print sources entirely. Printed materials (e.g., books, encyclopedias, journals, newspaper articles, pamphlets, brochures, and government publications) are indispensable sources for research on most topics. Unless you are instructed otherwise, use both print and Internet sources in any writing project that requires research. This chapter looks at issues you are likely to encounter when doing research on the Internet.

4a   Using Internet sources in your writing

Calling your readers' attention to Internet sources in your writing can give your work a special flair and distinction. However, if you use Internet sources, you must be careful to evaluate and cite them properly. When using and documenting Internet sources, follow three basic principles:

1. In your writing, make clear to readers which source you are referring to and how you understand its relevance to your topic.
2. Whatever citation style you use (MLA, APA, *Chicago*, or CBE), give your readers enough information to enable them to retrieve the source material if possible.
3. In your research notes or portfolio, store the data you collect about your Internet sources. Whether you store your notes and portfolio materials electronically, on paper, or both, you must preserve accurate data about your accessing of Internet sources. If possible, print out your Internet source bibliography whether you are required to or not.

As these three principles emphasize, you should pay careful attention to the details of reference citations. If you want readers to trust what you write, you must give them enough information to enable them to review your sources. Citing Internet sources is especially challenging because the Internet itself is constantly changing. New and different modes of access appear so frequently that pre-Internet documentation methods are often inadequate.

As information technology develops, new documentation conventions are needed. Chapters 5–8 of this book explain how to document online sources. For the latest information about citation, visit the **World Wide Web** site for *Online!* at <http://www.smpcollege.com/online -4styles~help>. If you have a question about your research, difficulty documenting a source, or trouble locating information, email us. We'll do all we can to help you find answers and solutions.

4b Identifying useful Internet sources

Finding sources of information on the Internet is relatively easy, but evaluating their quality requires great care. Searching the Internet with a tool such as Yahoo! or AltaVista, you're likely to get a list of potential sources whose quality and relevance varies greatly. The fact that a source is listed in a **subject directory**, linked to another Web page, or mentioned in an advertisement does not guarantee that it is reliable.

Deciding which Internet sources are most valuable for your project requires patience and practice because there are few, if any, standards regarding what may be published on the Web. Some computer system administrators and government agencies may try to restrict access to material they deem offensive. But such regulations, even if they could be enforced, would have no impact on the *truth* or *clarity* of claims expressed on the Internet.

Consider this: not only is there no editorial board for most Internet publications, there also is no market force to drive incompetent or untrustworthy publications off the Web. The democracy of the Internet is apparent from a Search Results screen, where each **hit** appears as important as all the rest.

Confronted by such anarchy, but knowing that *some* Internet information is reputable, you as a careful researcher should evaluate Internet sources by asking questions like these:

- Which sources are worth inspecting?
- What information is available about a given document?
- How should I represent my evaluation in my writing?

1 Deciding which sources are worth inspecting

The menus you generate by searching with the Internet tools discussed in Chapter 1 often stretch to many screens and include hundreds or thousands of items. The relevance of some items on the list may be obscure because the terms you searched for are located somewhere in the document's text and are not yet visible on your screen. After you open a document you can, of course, use your **browser**'s Find or Search function to see where in the text your **keywords** actually appear. Only as you examine the document can you begin to evaluate its usefulness and integrity.

Once you have a list of search results, create an entry on your **bookmark list** for the results screen so you can return to it easily. As you review the results, create additional **bookmarks** for useful-looking sites and documents. (See 4c-1 for more on bookmarks.)

2 Refining your search

To refine or limit your search, go to your **search tool**'s Help command (accessible directly from most search tools' screens). AltaVista's Help link, for example, suggests many ways to broaden or restrict searches. Suppose you want to explore Web sites offering information on transcultural adoption. A text search for such sites in August 1997 turned up more than 3,000 documents containing the word *transcultural* and nearly 200,000 documents containing the word *adoption*. When the search was narrowed to *transcultural adoption*, the query produced just twenty-two documents containing the phrase. When the search was further narrowed to look for the words *transcultural families* within those twenty-two documents, the field shrank to three documents—a very manageable number of sources to examine closely! While each search tool has its own means for refining or restricting a search, you should always be able to find a Help or Tips screen that explains the options.

3 Using additional search terms and search tools

If your search results are either too numerous for convenient reviewing or too few for your needs, see whether a closely related term produces more useful results. Using a wild-card technique (e.g., searching for *immigra** rather than *immigration*) usually generates more hits, while narrowing your topic by adding more search terms usually draws the most relevant hits to the top of the stack. You can also try a different search tool. (See 1g-2 for more on these tools.) Different search tools will give you different results, since each tool has its own strategy and its own database.

4c Gathering information about your Internet sources

Once you have assembled a list of useful sources, the next step is to gather the information you'll need to use the source. Capturing this information immediately is vital for finding it again and will make it easier to cite the source in your writing. Because Internet documents lack covers, dust jackets, and title pages, you'll have to inspect a source carefully for the information you need. Box 4.1 lists the types of information you should record.

1 Recording and bookmarking the information you collect

When working with print documents, you may be in the habit of recording essential bibliographic data either by hand or by photocopy. For Web, **gopher**, and **FTP** sources, much of the information you need is readily available while you are viewing a file, either on the screen or through browser menu selections. As you find useful sources on the Internet, develop the twin habits of (1) recording the document information for future reference, and (2) making a browser **bookmark** so that you can easily return to the source.

Recording the document information page   Depending on the programs you use, you may be able to store this data directly on your computer, or email it to yourself, or print it out. If your browser doesn't allow you to save the

---

Box 4.1
Information to record about an Internet source

Author(s)

Title of document

Electronic address

Date of publication

Date of access

Part or section heading or number

Other important information (e.g., type of email message)

document information to a file, open a wordprocessor window and use the copy-and-paste method to put the data into a file. Because a document's URL is crucial for your work, you must record it with absolute accuracy; therefore, any electronic means of storage or printing is preferable to handwriting. Be sure to record the date you access each URL. (See 4c-4 for help with finding URLs.)

Bookmarking the Web site   When you find a useful Web site, add a bookmark immediately. If you follow this practice, your bookmark list will grow into a complete index of your Internet sources, automatically recording much of the information you need for documentation. Your browser's menus give you access to the bookmarks file, which you can examine to find a source's title, its URL, and the date you accessed the bookmark.

If you share a computer with other users, your ability to make bookmarks may be limited, or you may worry that others will erase your bookmarks. Many graphic browsers let you save bookmarks from your current Web search to a file and later import them to the browser again. If so, you can carry your bookmarks on a floppy disk for security. Another, less convenient method is to use the copy-and-paste method to transfer URLs between your browser's screen and a text file in your computer.

2   Locating the correct title for a document

The most appropriate title for an Internet document is not always the heading that first gets your attention on the screen. Most graphic browsers show the document's actual title at the top of the screen window. Lynx displays the title in the upper right corner of the text window. If the onscreen title is obviously incomplete, or if you have doubts about its accuracy, look for the complete version in Netscape Navigator's Document Information window (which you can access from the View menu), in Microsoft Internet Explorer's Properties window (which you can access from the context menu with a click of the right mouse button), or by pressing = in Lynx. If the window title is uninformative or otherwise unsuitable, select the first main heading on the Web page.

Some documents are listed by search tools with the designation "no title" or with only a URL. If a document doesn't have a title, you will need to provide one so that you can find the document easily on your bookmark list and also cite it properly later. Avoid using "no title" and similar designations as titles of documents; instead, follow these rules of thumb:

- *If the untitled document contains text,* construct an appropriate title from the first major heading or the first text line. Enclose the title in square brackets to show that it is your editorial construction.

- *If the untitled document is a graphic,* construct a descriptive title such as "Photograph of Albert Einstein" and enclose it in square brackets.

- *If you reached the untitled document through a link,* you may be able to construct a title from the text surrounding the link. Record the title of the linking page for use with the citation format for **linkage data**.

- *If the untitled document is part of a larger hypertext work* (e.g., a chapter in a story), record the title of the complete work and then refer to the untitled source by its text division. Use this method when a source's URL contains a number sign (#), as in <http://www.spec tracom.com/islist/inet2.html#LITERATURE>, the Literature section of the Internet Services List.

3 Looking for the author(s) of a document

Authors of Internet documents don't always make their names readily visible. If the name of the person or organization responsible for an Internet source is not stated clearly at the beginning or end of the document, try the following approaches before labeling the source "anonymous":

- *Look for the author's email address.* If the address is not clearly visible, use your browser's Find or Search function to locate the @ symbol (which appears in every Internet email address).

- *Open the document's Source Information window,* which you access from the View menu in a graphic browser or by pressing \ (the backslash key) in Lynx. Look for lines that specify the "owner" of the document, and record any names or email addresses you find.

- *If you locate an email address but no personal name,* try to find the real name by "fingering" the address. *Finger* is an Internet function that may be available from your system prompt (if you have **indirect access** to the Internet), from software on your own computer, or through a Web site such as <http//www.cs.indiana .edu/finger>. Finger and similar tools let you match names with email addresses. For more information about using finger, see Andrew Starr's Web page at <http://www.amherst.edu/~atstarr/computers /finger.html>. While the information from finger and other such tools is generally reliable, remember that some Internet-connected systems don't respond to finger requests and some systems use email address-es that won't work with these search tools.

4 Finding a document's URL

Every Internet document has a unique "address," or **URL (uniform resource locator)**, which specifies how the document can be retrieved. Graphic browsers usually display the current URL in a window. Some printer settings let you record the URL on each printed page of text. But the easiest way to find and record a document's URL is to use your browser's bookmark feature (described in 2a and 4c-1). Use the URL recorded with your bookmark unless you decide to shorten it (see the following section, "Shortening URLS").

The URL for a **telnet** session can't be captured through your browser's bookmark menu, but you can record it by opening the **context menu** (e.g., by clicking the right mouse button) for the telnet link and selecting "Add Bookmark." In Lynx, highlight the telnet link, press the = key, and record the URL by hand.

Shortening URLs In a URL, any material following # (the number sign) represents a section or division of a single file. If you're producing printed text and want to minimize the number of long URLs you show in the text, you can shorten a URL by ending it at the # sign and using the section label as a text division (as you would the page number of a printed book). For example, the URL

▶ <http://www.spectracom.com/islist/inet2.html# LITERATURE>

can be simplified to

▶ `<http://www.spectracom.com/islist/inet2.html>`

if you tell your readers that you're referring to the LITERATURE section of this document.

Very complicated or long URLs can be shortened (and the retrieval process simplified for your readers) if you can supply enough information about the source through **linkage data** notes. For example, the complete URL for "Pentium Jokes" at `<gopher://utserv.utoledo.edu:70 /00GOPHER_ROOT%3a%5b000000.ENTERTAIN MENT.JOKES-STORIES-AND-MORE.COMPUTER -RELATED-MATERIAL%5dPENTIUM.JOKES>` can be shortened to `<gopher://utserv.utoledo.edu>` if you specify that the joke list is "Lkd. 'Gopher Menu,' at 'Internet Activities,' 'Entertainment,' 'Jokes,' and 'Com-puter-Related Material." Identifying and specifying alternate paths is not always simple, particularly for gopher items, but it can make your (printed) text more readable.

Typing URLs For rules about typing URLs, see 1d-2.

5 Working with frames

Many Web pages contain two or more **frames**. Frames let you see and work with several documents in one screen window. For example, a page might show the table of contents for a book in one frame and the text in another frame. Selecting a link in one frame sometimes changes the display in another frame, but the window, title, and general layout usually remain unchanged. Figure 4.1 (on page 62) shows a page with three frames.

Most frames are easily recognized by scroll bars at the frames' edges that give you control over what you see. In other cases, the best evidence that you're working with frames is that the URL in the dialog box remains unchanged as you click links and watch new informa-tion appear in various regions of the window. (If a link inside a frame leads you to a different site or a different part of the same site, the URL will of course change.)

You need to know about frames in order to

• Print what you see in a frame

• Create bookmarks for frames

• Refer accurately to framed information

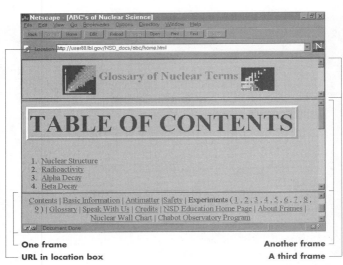

One frame   Another frame

URL in location box   A third frame

Figure 4.1
A page containing three frames, each with its own scroll bar
<http://user88.lbl.gov/NSD_docs/abc/home.html>

Printing a frame To print the information from a frame, you must first make that frame "active" by clicking inside its borders. If you click somewhere else, your printout may not contain what you really wanted.

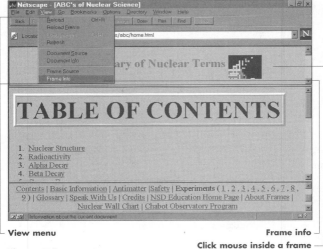

View menu   Frame info

                             Click mouse inside a frame

Figure 4.2
Selecting the Frame Info window

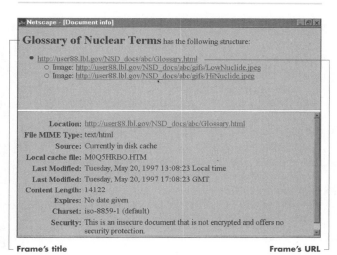

Frame's title   Frame's URL

Figure 4.3
The Frame Info window for one of the frames shown in
Figure 4.1

Bookmarking a frame Adding bookmarks for pages
containing frames can be tricky. Your browser's menu
option always records just the main page's URL, ignor-
ing your selections in any frames. To add a Netscape
bookmark for the information inside a frame, click
inside the frame and then open the View menu. Select
"Frame Info," and in that window use your mouse to
right-click (with Windows 95) or **click-and-hold** (with
Macintosh) at the URL. Select "Add Bookmark" from
the resulting menu. (See Figures 4.2–4.4.) To add an
Internet Explorer **favorite** for a frame, open the frame's
context menu (e.g., by right-clicking the mouse in the
frame) and select "Add to Favorites." When you use
such a bookmark, your browser will open it in its own
window; that is, you won't see other frames from the
original site.

Referring to information inside a frame To refer accurately to the information inside a frame, you have two
options: you can use the **linkage data** citation format
(defined in 5b-10, 6b-10, 7b-10, and 8b-10) with the main
page's URL, or you can cite the frame like an ordinary
Web page (see 5b-1, 6b-1, 7b-1, and 8b-1) using the
frame's own URL. The URL displayed in the dialog box
gives the address for the whole page you are viewing; it

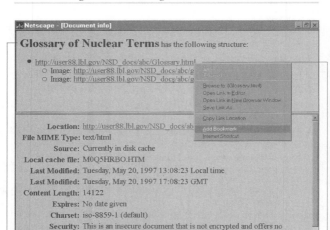

Frame's title   Frame's URL

Figure 4.4
Using the context menu to add a bookmark for a frame

doesn't point uniquely to any specific frame inside. You can find the active frame's URL from Netscape's Frame Info window (as shown in Figure 4.3). To get the URL from Internet Explorer, open the frame's context menu and select "Properties." (See Figures 4.5 and 4.6.)

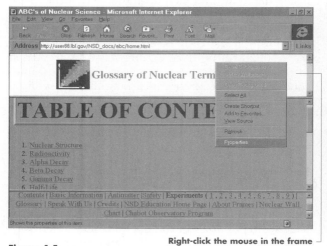

Right-click the mouse in the frame

Figure 4.5
Selecting the Properties window from Microsoft Internet Explorer

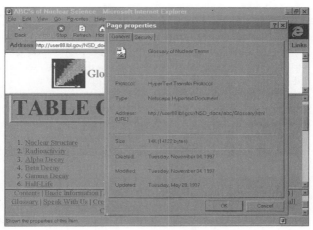

Figure 4.6
A Properties window in Microsoft Internet Explorer

6 Keeping track of publication and access dates

Keep track of two dates associated with your Internet sources:

- Publication date (sometimes listed as *revision* or *modification* date)
- Access date

An Internet document's *date of publication* is essential for identifying the document, since a file with a given title can be changed or replaced without a trace. Many Internet authors include a publication date (or a date of *last revision* or *modification*) prominently at the top or bottom of a page.

The *date of access* tells readers when you accessed the document. This date, which usually differs from the publication date, becomes very important when you want to quote from the source or use its data. When you state your access date, you are claiming that the document as reported was available at that particular time. But a document may later be revised or cease to be available. Consider this scenario: you cite a source with a "last revision" date of December 31, 1996. If the author revises the file and simultaneously updates the revision date, others using your citation to locate the file will find a different date and will thus know they're looking at a changed file.

Your browser may provide convenient methods for recording access dates. For example, Netscape Navigator automatically stores the creation and access dates for each bookmark. You can find these dates by opening the Bookmarks file from the Window menu, highlighting a bookmark, and then opening the Item — Properties window.

Occasionally — for example, when looking at a directory obtained through FTP — you will come across a document's *file date*. The file date represents the date the document was stored on a particular computer. It is *not* the same as the date of publication.

Some search tools — notably AltaVista — associate a date with each item found during a search. These dates show how recently the site was indexed by the search tool; again, they do *not* reflect the item's publication date. Always look for the publication date of an Internet source inside the document or on the Document Information page.

Be sure to record a document's publication and access dates as accurately as possible.

7 Understanding site ratings

Various organizations such as Magellan at <http://www.mckinley.com> and Lycos at <http://www.lycos.com> offer ratings of Web sites. These ratings and other "awards" are often featured on the rated pages themselves. Don't let a rating claim interfere (positively or negatively) with your judgment of a site's reliability unless you understand clearly how the rating is done. Ratings often focus primarily on the presentation and organization of the information rather than on its reliability. For example, Lycos gives its Top 5% award to Web sites that qualify according to the following standards (listed under "What are the rating categories?" in Lycos's Help at <http://www.lycos.com/help/top5-help2.html>):

> *Content:* The content rating indicates how informative the site is. Does it cover its topic in a broad, deep, and thorough manner? Is the information useful, accurate, and up-to-date?

> *Design:* The design rating assesses the site's layout and presentation. Does it lead visitors through the information

nicely? Are the pages beautiful, colorful, and easy to use? Does the site use video, audio, and original graphics?

Overall: The overall rating combines the content and design metrics with criteria such as amusement, personality, and charm. Is the site fun, inviting, and captivating? Would you like to meet the people behind the site?

An award that emphasizes how much "fun" a site might be should not be taken as evidence that the source's content has been evaluated thoroughly.

Several site rating systems have recently been designed to help parents and other authorities cope with growing concerns about obscenity, pornography, and profanity on the Web. The best known of these is the RSACI system, developed by the Recreational Software Advisory Council on the Internet, which defines five levels of intensity in each of four categories (violence,

Figure 4.7
A guide rating page from The Argus Clearinghouse
<http://www.clearinghouse.net>

nudity, sex, and language) to describe what a user might encounter at a particular Web site. You can find detailed descriptions for these criteria and their use at <http://www.rsac.org>. Although these ratings may be useful in certain circumstances, their characterization of the moral or psychological orientation of a site's material does not rate the *reliability* of the site's content.

By contrast, the very helpful ratings offered by The Argus Clearinghouse at <http://www.clearinghouse .net> are specifically content-oriented. Although The Clearinghouse librarians review only **subject guides** (webliographies), not individual Web sites, The Clearing-house approval means that a particular subject guide is likely to include worthwhile critiques of important resources. The Clearinghouse rating for a typical (excellent) subject guide is shown in Figure 4.7. Note that the rating date is specified, and that five criteria are used:

- Level of resource description
- Level of resource evaluation
- Guide design
- Guide organizational schemes
- Guide meta-information

The Clearinghouse provides detailed explanations for these criteria at <http://www.clearinghouse.net/ratings .html>.

4d   Evaluating the reliability of an Internet source

Paul Gilster in *Digital Literacy*[1] maintains that "while the Internet offers myriad opportunities for learning, an unconsidered view of its contents can be misleading and deceptive. . . . You cannot work comfortably within this medium until you have established methods for judging the reliability of Web pages, newsgroup postings, and mailing lists" (87). Gilster's point about the necessity of personal involvement—that *you* must become proficient in judging reliability on the Web—

---

[1] Gilster, Paul. *Digital Literacy.* New York: Wiley, 1997. See also Paul Gilster, *A Primer on Digital Literacy,* 17 Nov. 1997, Wiley, 24 Nov. 1997 <http://metalab.unc.edu/cisco/noc/primer.html>.

cannot be overemphasized. Critical evaluation of Web sources is a daily, unending task *for each user* because the Web's design promotes change and reconstruction — a new link here, a typing error corrected there — which effectively prevents fixed judgments.

But you are not helpless and alone! The Web contains a growing number of documents to help you evaluate the sources you encounter. Links to many of these documents can be found in the subject guide "Evaluation of Information Sources" by Alastair Smith at <http://www.vuw.ac.nz/~agsmith/evaln/evaln.htm>. One of the best summaries of the evaluation process is Elizabeth Kirk's document "Evaluating Information Found on the Internet" at <http://milton.mse.jhu.edu:8001/research/education/net.html>. Kirk identifies five major criteria for evaluating all forms of information:

- Authorship
- Publishing body
- Knowledge of other sources
- Accuracy or verifiability
- Currency

The following sections describe these criteria in detail; 4d-6 points to a "checklist" method for carrying out an evaluation.

1 Authorship

To find out more about the *authorship* of an Internet document, consider searching for the author's name on the Web or in Usenet. (With AltaVista, for example, you simply type in the author's name and request a Web or Usenet search for text containing information. If the author maintains a homepage, it will be listed.) If biographical links are available, follow them; if the author encourages contact via email, consider the offer seriously. Most Web authors appreciate hearing from people who make use of their information, and the Internet provides a mechanism for responding that most print publications cannot match. An author's homepage may contain helpful information, but comments from others about the author's work are useful as well. Your goal is to establish the author's qualifications for making the claims you want to use.

2 Publishing body

The *publishing body* for an Internet document is the **server** on which the file is stored, but there is no way for the server to guarantee the reliability of the information it stores. More important than the server's name are any names or logos appearing within the document that represent organizations that may stand behind the author's work. For example, you can be confident that Leslie Harris's essay "Writing Spaces: Using MOOs to Teach Composition and Literature," which appeared in *Kairos: A Journal for Teaching Writing in Webbed Environments* (Summer 1996), is valuable. *Kairos,* an electronic journal sponsored by the Alliance for Computers and Writing at <http://english.ttu.edu/kairos>, has an international reputation for publishing articles of high quality.

3 Referral to and/or knowledge of other sources

Understanding the author's *"referral to and/or knowledge of other sources"* is probably the key to estimating the reliability of Internet source material. To find evidence that will help you make this judgment, you can use two approaches:

1. Examine the content of the document to see whether it represents other sources fairly.
2. Seek out other sources to see if the author has considered enough alternative views.

Of course, you may need guidance from others in the author's field in order to make an informed judgment. Here the Internet can play a key role by enabling you to search quickly for the names or ideas of others mentioned by the author. For example, you might subscribe to a **listserv** or participate in a **newsgroup** in the author's field, both to learn more about the context of the author's work and to be able to seek others' opinions if necessary.

4 Accuracy or verifiability

How you establish the *accuracy* of data you find on the Internet is not very different from how you establish the accuracy of print data, but the special features of **hypertext** often make your task easier. For example, an author quoting statistics from another Internet source will often include a direct link to the other source. Even though Internet sources that point to other documents in this fashion may not have traditional bibliographies, they are nonetheless well documented.

5 Currency

The *currency* of an Internet document refers to the history of its publication and any revisions. A document with no dating at all is less reliable (on this particular score) than one that lists numerous revisions; in the second case, the author shows greater respect for readers' information needs.

6 Checklists for evaluating sources

Another good source for evaluation techniques is the "Web Evaluation Menu" from Widener University at <http://www.science.widener.edu/~withers/webeval .htm>. This site offers a step-by-step approach to evaluating a Web site's authority, accuracy, objectivity, currency, and coverage. Checklists for five different categories of Web sites (business, reference, news, advocacy, and personal pages) provide detailed questions to answer. Each checklist focuses on verifying the legitimacy of the information and its sponsoring organization or individual(s). This highly structured approach differs from the more intuitive practice described in 4d-1 through 4d-5, but the resulting evaluations of a Web site's reliability will be essentially the same. Use whichever method you prefer!

4e Representing your evaluation in your writing

When you use an Internet source in your writing, demonstrate your evaluation of the source's reliability by carefully choosing a *signal verb* to show your understanding of the author's purpose (what the author is trying to achieve in his or her writing) and how successful the author is in achieving that purpose. By using signal verbs, you let readers know the context in which the source's statement should be viewed.

Consider the following quotation from a message that Jeremy Abrams posted in 1996 to the newsgroup <alt.philosophy.objectivism>:

> Science offers no substitute for the ethical concern of religion.

You can introduce your use of this quotation with a variety of signal verbs:

> Jeremy Abrams *says* that . . .
>
> Jeremy Abrams *believes* that . . .
>
> Jeremy Abrams *claims* that . . .
>
> Jeremy Abrams *argues* that . . .
>
> Jeremy Abrams *proves* that . . .

Your choice of the signal verb helps your reader understand both Abrams's intention and the degree to which he affirms and supports his statements. If you choose to use *proves* instead of *believes*, then you signal to your reader that the quotation in context proves by convincing evidence and persuasive logic that "science offers no substitute for the ethical concern of religion." If you choose the signal verb *say* instead of *prove*, you are reporting that Abrams makes his statement without any substantial support. Choose your signal verbs carefully

---

Box 4.2
Signal verbs for evaluating sources

acknowledges	discusses	recognizes
advises	embraces	regards
agrees	emphasizes	remarks
allows	explains	replies
analyzes	expresses	reports
answers	holds	responds
appreciates	implies	reveals
asserts	interprets	says
assumes	leaves us with	states
believes	lists	suggests
charges	objects	supports
claims	observes	tells us
considers	offers	thinks
criticizes	opposes	wants to
declares	points to	wishes
describes	presents	wonders
disagrees	proposes	

so that they genuinely reflect the tone and substance of each cited source.

Box 4.2 lists some signal verbs you can use to show your readers how you have evaluated your sources. By using signal verbs to introduce and discuss Internet and print sources, you add integrity to your authorial voice and encourage your readers to trust the judgments you make in reporting and evaluating information.

Chapters 5 through 8 provide guidelines for citing and documenting Internet sources in four widely used styles. If you are required to follow a citation style not discussed here, and if that style doesn't cover Internet sources, you can adapt the style to fit the Internet sources you need to cite (using 6a, 7a, and 8a as a guide) and then ask your instructor or editor to review your adaptation.

CHAPTER FIVE

Using MLA Style to Cite and Document Sources

This chapter's guidelines for citing Internet sources are based on two sources: the *MLA Handbook for Writers of Research Papers* (1995) by Joseph Gibaldi, and the Modern Language Association of America (MLA) Web site at <http://www.mla.org/main_stl.htm#sources>, which provides sample Works Cited entries for some common kinds of World Wide Web sources. The *MLA Handbook* advises that you acknowledge sources "by keying brief parenthetical citations in your text to an alphabetical list of works that appears at the end of the paper" (xiii). Widely used by writers in literature, language studies, and other fields in the humanities, the MLA style of documentation allows writers to keep texts "as readable and as free of disruptions as possible" (105).

The *MLA Handbook* provides information about the purposes of research; suggestions for choosing topics; recommendations for using libraries; guidance for composing outlines, drafts, notes, and bibliographies; and advice on spelling, punctuation, abbreviations, and other stylistic matters. It also presents a style for documenting sources and gives directions for citing print sources in the text and preparing a list of Works Cited. Thorough acquaintance with the *MLA Handbook* will, as its author promises, "help you become a writer whose work deserves serious consideration" (xiii). This chapter follows the conventions of MLA citation style.

5a Using principles of MLA style to cite Internet sources

The *MLA Handbook* gives guidelines for making in-text references to print sources. The following section shows how you can apply the same principles to citing online sources in your text.

1 Link an in-text citation of an Internet source to a corresponding entry in the Works Cited.

According to the *MLA Handbook*, each text reference to an outside source must point clearly to a specific entry in the list of Works Cited. The essential elements of an in-text citation are the author's name (or the document's title, if no author is identified) and a page reference or other information showing where in a source cited material appears.

Create an in-text reference to an Internet source by using a signal phrase, a parenthetical citation, or both a previewing sentence and a parenthetical citation.

Box 5.1
Using italics and underlining in MLA style

MLA style recommends italicizing certain elements (e.g., book and journal titles) in printed text and underlining them in manuscript. The use of underlining to represent italics becomes a problem when you compose texts for online publication. On the World Wide Web, underlining in a document indicates that the under-lined word or phrase is an active hypertext link. (All HTML editing programs automatically underline any text linked to another hyper-text or Web site.)

When composing Web documents, avoid underlining. Instead, use italics for titles, for emphasis, and for words, letters, and numbers referred to as such. When you write with programs such as email that don't allow italics, type an underscore mark _like this_ before and after text you would otherwise italicize or underline.

Using a signal phrase To introduce cited material consisting of a short quotation, paraphrase, or summary, use either a signal phrase set off by a comma or a signal verb with a *that* clause, as in the following examples. (See 4e for a discussion of signal phrases and verbs.)

> **signal phrase**
>
> ▶ According to Steven E. Landsburg, "if you know you're going to treasure something, you don't hesitate to buy it."

> **signal phrase**
>
> ▶ In his January 1991 letter to the editors of PMLA, Jason Mitchell suggests that the "pretentious gibberish" of modern literary critics-- "Eurojive," as he calls it--is often produced by English professors who need to prove that their professional status is equal to that of math and science faculty.

Here are the Works Cited entries for these two sources:

▶ Landsburg, Steven E. "Who Shall Inherit the
    Earth?" Slate 1 May 1997. 2 May 1997
    <http://www.slate.com/Economics/97-05-01
    /Economics.asp>.

▶ Mitchell, Jason P. "PMLA Letter." 1991. 23 May
    1996 <http://sunset.backbone.olemiss.edu
    /~jmitchel/pmla.htm>.

Using a parenthetical citation To identify the source of a quotation, paraphrase, or summary, place the author's last name in parentheses after the cited material.

▶ "Parents know in advance, and with near cer-
    tainty, that they will be addicted to their
    children" (Landsburg).

▶ In response to Victor Brombert's 1990 MLA pres-
    idential address on the "politics of critical
    language," one correspondent suggests that "some
    literary scholars envy the scientists their
    wonderful jargon with its certainty and preci-

sion and thus wish to emulate it by creating
formidably technical-sounding words of their
own" (Mitchell).

Here are the Works Cited entries for these sources:

▶ Landsburg, Steven E. "Who Shall Inherit the
   Earth?" <u>Slate</u> 1 May 1997. 2 May 1997
   <http://www.slate.com/Economics/97-05-01
   /Economics.asp>.

▶ Mitchell, Jason P. "PMLA Letter." 1991. 23 May
   1996 <http://sunset.backbone.olemiss.edu
   /~jmitchel/pmla.htm>.

Using a previewing sentence and a parenthetical citation
To introduce and identify the source of a long quotation
(one comprising more than four lines in your essay or
research paper), use a previewing sentence that ends in
a colon. By briefly announcing the content of an extended quotation, a previewing sentence tells readers what
to look for in the quotation. Indent the block quotation
ten spaces (or two paragraph indents) from the left margin. At the end of the block quotation, cite the source in
parentheses after the final punctuation mark.

▶ That the heroic and historically important
   deeds of previously unknown women should be
   included in history books is evident from the
   following notice:

        Event: April 26, 1777, Sybil Ludington.
        On the night of April 26, 1777, Sybil
        Ludington, age 16, rode through towns in
        New York and Connecticut to warn that the
        Redcoats were coming . . . to Danbury,
        CT. All very Paul Reverish, except Sybil
        completed HER ride, and SHE thus gathered
        enough volunteers to help beat back the
        British the next day. Her ride was twice
        the distance of Revere's. No poet immor-
        talized (and faked) her accomplishments,
        but at least her hometown was renamed
        after her. However, recently the National
        Rifle Association established a Sybil
        Ludington women's "freedom" award for mer-
        itorious service in furthering the purpos-
        es of the NRA as well as use of firearms

> in competition or in actual life-threaten-
> ing situations although Sybil never fired
> a gun. (Stuber)

Here is the Works Cited entry:

▶ Stuber, Irene. "April 26, 1996: Episode 638."
  <u>Women of Achievement and Herstory: A
  Frequently-Appearing Newsletter</u>. 3 May
  1996. 11 Dec. 1997 <http://www.imageworld
  .com/vsp/istuber/woa/1996/woa638.asc>.

2 Substitute Internet text divisions for page numbers.

The examples in 5a-1 assume that an Internet source has
no internal divisions (pages, parts, chapters, headings,
sections, subsections). The *MLA Handbook*, however,
requires that you identify the location of any cited information as precisely as possible in parentheses. Because
Internet sources are rarely marked with page numbers,
you will not always be able to show exactly where cited
material comes from. If a source has internal divisions,
use these instead of page numbers in your citation. Be
sure to use divisions inherent in the document and not
those provided by your browsing software.

A text reference to a source with divisions may appear
in the text along with the author's name or be placed in
parentheses after a quotation, paraphrase, or summary.

▶ As TyAnna Herrington notes in her Introduction,
  "Nicholas Negroponte's <u>Being Digital</u> provides
  another welcome not only into an age of technological ubiquity, but into a way of 'being'
  with technology."

▶ "Negroponte's uncomplicated, personal tone fools
  the reader into a sense that his theses are
  simplistic" (Herrington "Introduction").

Here is the Works Cited entry:

▶ Herrington, TyAnna K. "Being Is Believing."
      Rev. of <u>Being Digital</u>, by Nicholas
      Negroponte. Lkd. <u>Kairos: A Journal for
      Teaching Writing in Webbed Environments</u>
      1.1 (1996) at "Reviews." 24 May 1996
      <http://english.ttu.edu/kairos/1.1>.

3 Use source-reflective statements to show where cited material ends.

The MLA practice of parenthetical page-number citation lets you indicate precisely where information from a printed source ends. Many Internet sources, however, appear as single screens, and MLA style does not require parenthetical page citations for one-page works. By analogy, a single-screen document cited in text needs no page citation. To let your readers know where your use of an Internet source with no text divisions ends, use a source-reflective statement.

Source-reflective statements give you an opportunity to assert your authorial voice. Writers use source-reflective statements to provide editorial comment, clarification, qualification, amplification, dissent, agreement, and so on. In the following example, the absence of a source-reflective statement creates uncertainty as to where use of an Internet source ends.

▶ According to TyAnna Herrington, Nicholas
   Negroponte has the ability to make complex
   technological issues understandably simple.
   For those who are not techno-philes, this is a
   blessing; it allows them to apprehend the real
   significance of digital technology without
   feeling that such ideas are too difficult to
   consider.

In the next example, the writer has added a source-reflective statement to show that use of the source has ended.

source-reflective statement

▶ According to TyAnna Herrington, Nicholas
   Negroponte has the ability to make complex
   technological issues understandably simple.
   Herrington's observation is a good one.
   It means that for those who are not techno-
   philes, reading Negroponte is a blessing; reading Negroponte allows one to apprehend the real
   significance of digital technology without
   feeling that such ideas are too difficult to
   consider.

Here is the Works Cited entry:

▶ Herrington, TyAnna K. "Being Is Believing."
      Rev. of <u>Being Digital</u>, by Nicholas
      Negroponte. Lkd. <u>Kairos: A Journal for
      Teaching Writing in Webbed Environments</u>
      1.1 (1996) at "Reviews." 24 May 1996
      <http://english.ttu.edu/kairos/1.1>.

5b Works Cited

When using MLA style, place a list of cited sources, arranged alphabetically, after the text of your essay and any explanatory notes. The *MLA Handbook* recommends that you "draft the [Works Cited] section in advance, so that you will know what information to give in parenthetical references as you write" (106). Doing this makes in-text citation of sources easier by giving you an idea of what in-text reference options will work best for each citation.

Referring to print sources, the *MLA Handbook* gives the following general models for Works Cited entries:

Book

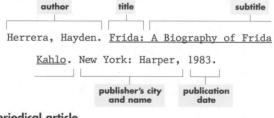

Periodical article

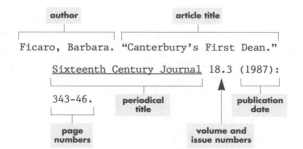

Box 5.2
Using hypertext to document sources on the Web

The hypertext environment of the World Wide Web doesn't just alter the way you do research, it also lets you document sources in a new way—by using hypertext links. Electronic journals published on the Web are already replacing traditional notes, Works Cited listings, appendixes, and other supporting text with links to the documents being cited. To read more about hypertext documentation, see Chapter 10 in this book. For an example of how it works, look at the format of Andrew Harnack and Eugene Kleppinger, "Beyond the *MLA Handbook:* Documenting Electronic Sources on the Internet" in *Kairos: A Journal for Teaching Writing in Webbed Environments* 1.2 (1996) at <http://english.ttu.edu /kairos/1.2/inbox/mla.html> or any essay published in *Kairos* at <http://english.ttu.edu/kairos>.

The *MLA Handbook* also presents numerous variations that accommodate a variety of print sources (e.g., a multivolume work, an editorial). For detailed information on creating a Works Cited list, see Chapter 4 of the *MLA Handbook,* "Documentation: Preparing the List of Works Cited."

In addition to recommendations in the *MLA Handbook,* MLA guidelines for some online sources are posted on the World Wide Web at <http://www.mla.org/main_stl .htm#sources>. When you document sources from the Web, the MLA suggests that your Works Cited entries contain as many items from the following list as are relevant and available:

1. Name of the author, editor, compiler, or translator (if available and relevant), alphabetized by last name and followed by any appropriate abbreviations, such as *ed.*
2. Title of a poem, short story, article, or other short work within a scholarly project, database, or periodical (in quotation marks), or title of a posting to a discussion list or forum (taken from the subject line, put in quotation marks, and followed by the description *online posting)*
3. Title of a book (underlined)
4. Name of the editor, compiler, or translator (if relevant and if not cited earlier), preceded by any appropriate abbreviation, such as *ed.*
5. Publication information for any print version
6. Title of the scholarly project, database, periodical, or professional or personal site (underlined), or, for a

professional or personal site with no title, a description such as *home page*[1]

7. Name of the editor of a scholarly project or database (if available)
8. Version number (if not part of the title) or, for a journal, the volume, issue, or other identifying number
9. For a posting to a discussion list, the name of the list or forum
10. Date of electronic publication, latest update, or posting, whichever is latest (if known; otherwise use *n.d.)*
11. Number of pages, paragraphs, or other identifiable sections (if any)
12. Name of any institution or organization sponsoring or associated with the Web site
13. Date you accessed the source
14. URL (in angle brackets)

Although no single entry will contain all fourteen items of information, all Works Cited entries for Web sources contain the following basic information:

Online document

▶ Author's name (last name first). Document
        title. Date of Internet publication.
        Date of access <URL>.

Current MLA guidelines for citing Internet documents focus on the World Wide Web. The MLA guidelines don't provide specific or detailed advice on how to cite **email** or **newsgroup** messages; **listserv** messages not accessed via the Web; **real-time communications**; **telnet** sites; **FTP** sites; **gopher** sites; **linkage data**; or **frames**. Sometimes it may be helpful to your readers to include more information than the MLA guidelines require. For example, providing the author's email address after the author's name with certain online sources—email messages, **Web discussion forums**, and listserv and newsgroup postings—allows readers to authenticate the source if necessary. The following models, based on citation principles in the *MLA Handbook* and on sample entries for some common kinds of Web sources at MLA's Web site <http://www.mla.org/main_stl.htm#sources>, enable you to document all Internet sources in a manner consistent with MLA style.

---

[1] *Home page* is the spelling that MLA currently recommends.

Box 5.3
Formatting Works Cited entries in HTML

Some HTML editors don't let you easily indent the second line of a Works Cited entry. In such instances, bullet the first line of an entry.

- Landsburg, Steven E. "Who Shall Inherit
  the Earth?" <u>Slate</u> 1 May 1997. 2 May 1997
  <http://www.slate.com/Economics/97-05-01
  /Economics.asp>.

- Mitchell, Jason P. "PMLA Letter." 1991. 23
  May 1996 <http://sunset.backbone.olemiss.edu
  /~jmitchel/pmla.htm>.

1 World Wide Web site

To document a file available for viewing and download-ing via the **World Wide Web**, provide the following information:

- author's name (if known)
- title of document, in quotation marks
- title of complete work (if applicable), in italics or underlined
- site description (if applicable)
- date of publication or last revision (if known)
- date of access
- URL, in angle brackets

Personal site

▶ Pellegrino, Joseph. Home page. 24 Sept. 1997.
  7 Nov. 1997 <http://www.english.eku.edu
  /pellegri/personal.htm>.

General Web site

▶ Harris, Jonathan G. "The Return of the Witch
  Hunts." <u>Witchhunt Information Page</u>. 19
  Apr. 1997. 19 Nov. 1997 <http://web.mit
  .edu/harris/www/fells.short.html>.

▶ Shade, Leslie R. "Gender Issues in Computer
  Networking." 14 Feb. 1994. 26 Nov. 1997
  <http://www.mit.edu:8001/people/sorokin
  /women/lrs.html>.

Book

▶ Darwin, Charles. <u>The Voyage of the</u> Beagle.
    London, 1845. <u>Project Gutenberg</u>. June
    1997. 1 Oct. 1997 <ftp://uiarchive.cso
    .uiuc.edu/pub/etext/gutenberg/etext97
    /vbgle10.txt>.

Article in an electronic journal (ejournal)

▶ Browning, Tonya. "Embedded Visuals: Student
    Design in Web Spaces." <u>Kairos: A Journal
    for Teachers of Writing in Webbed Environ-
    ments</u> 2.1 (1997). 21 Oct. 1997 <http://
    english.ttu.edu/kairos/2.1/features
    /browning>.

Article in an electronic magazine (ezine)

▶ Myhrvold, Nathan. "Confessions of a
    Cybershaman." <u>Slate</u> 12 June 1997. 19 Oct.
    1997 <http://www.slate.com/CriticalMass
    /97-06-12/CriticalMass.asp>.

Government publication

▶ Bush, George. "Principles of Ethical Conduct
    for Government Officers and Employees."
    Executive Order 12674 of April 12, 1989
    (as modified by E. O. 12731). Part 1.
    26 Aug. 1997. 18 Nov. 1997 <http://www
    .usoge.gov/exorders/eo12674.html>.

To cite information appearing in a **frame** within a larger
Web document, use the guidelines in 5b-10 for **linkage
data**.

2 Email message

To document an **email** message, provide the following
information:

- author's name (if known)
- author's email address, in angle brackets
- subject line from posting, in quotation marks
- type of communication (personal email, distribution
  list, office communication)
- date of publication
- date of access

▶ Franke, Norman. <frankel@llnl.gov> "SoundApp
    2.0.2." Personal email. 29 Apr. 1996.
    3 May 1996.

▶ Robinette, Danny. <robinetted@ccmail.gate.eku
    .edu> "Epiphany Project." Office communi-
    cation. 30 Apr. 1996. 29 May 1996.

3 Web discussion forum posting

To document a posting to a **Web discussion forum**, provide the following information:

- author's name
- author's email address, in angle brackets
- subject line or title of posting, in quotation marks
- type of message (if appropriate)
- date of publication
- date of access
- URL, in angle brackets

▶ LaLiberte, Daniel. <liberte@ncsa.uiuc.edu>
    "HyperNews Instructions." Online posting.
    23 May 1996. 24 May 1996 <http://union
    .ncsa.uiuc.edu/HyperNews/get/hypernews
    /instructions.html>.

▶ Saffran, Art. <saffran@wisbar.org> "It's Not
    That Hard." Online posting. 5 Jan. 1996.
    24 May 1996 <http://union.ncsa.uiuc.edu
    /HyperNews/get/hypernews/instructions
    /90/1/1.html>.

4 Listserv message

To document a **listserv** message, provide the following
information:

- author's name (if known)
- author's email address, in angle brackets
- subject line from posting, in quotation marks
- date of publication
- date of access
- address of listserv, in angle brackets

▶ Parente, Victor. <vrparent@mailbox.syr.edu> "On
    Expectations of Class Participation." 27 May
    1996. 29 May 1996 <philosed@sued.syr.edu>.

To document a file that can be retrieved from a list's
server or Web address, provide the following information after the subject line:

- phrase *online posting*
- date of publication
- date of access
- address of listserv, in angle brackets
- address or URL for list's archive, preceded by *via* and
  enclosed in angle brackets

▶ Carbone, Nick. <nickc@english.umass.edu> "NN
    960126: Followup to Don's Comments about
    Citing URLs." Online posting. 26 Jan. 1996.
    17 Feb. 1996 <acw-l@unicorn.acs.ttu.edu>
    via <http://www.ttu.edu/lists/acw-l>.

5 Newsgroup message

To document information posted in a **newsgroup** discussion, provide the following information:

- author's name (if known)
- author's email address, in angle brackets
- subject line from posting, in quotation marks
- date of publication
- date of access
- name of newsgroup, in angle brackets

▶ Slade, Robert. <res@maths.bath.ac.uk> "UNIX Made
    Easy." 26 Mar. 1996. 31 Mar. 1996 <alt
    .books.reviews>.

If, after following all the suggestions in 4c-3, you cannot
determine the author's name, then use the author's
email address, enclosed in angle brackets, as the main
entry. When you alphabetize such sources in your Works
Cited, treat the first letter of the email address as though
it were capitalized.

▶ <lrm583@aol.com> "Thinking of Adoption." 26 May
    1996. 29 May 1996 <alt.adoption>.

6 Real-time communication

To document a **real-time communication**, such as those posted in **MOOs**, **MUDs**, and **IRCs**, provide the following information:

- name of speaker(s) (if known), or name of site
- title of event (if appropriate), in quotation marks
- type of communication (group discussion, personal interview), if not indicated elsewhere in entry
- date of event
- date of access
- address, using a URL (in angle brackets) or command-line directions

▶ LambdaMOO. "Seminar Discussion on Netiquette."
     28 May 1996. 28 May 1996 <telnet://lambda
     .parc.xerox.edu:8888>.

▶ Harnack, Andrew. "Words." Group discussion. 4
     Apr. 1996. 5 Apr. 1996 telnet moo.du.org
     /port=8888.

7 Telnet site

To document a **telnet** site or a file available via telnet, provide the following information:

- author's name (if known)
- title of document (if known), in quotation marks
- title of full work (if applicable), in italics or underlined
- date of publication (if known)
- date of access
- word *telnet*
- complete telnet address
- directions for accessing document

▶ Aquatic Conservation Network. "About the
     Aquatic Conservation Network." National
     Capital Freenet. N.d. 28 May 1996 telnet
     freenet.carleton.ca login as guest, go
     acn, press 1.

▶ California Department of Pesticide Regulation.
     "Pest Management Information." CSU Fresno

> <u>ATI-NET</u>. N.d. 28 May 1996 telnet caticsuf
> .csufresno.edu login as super, press a,
> press k.

8 FTP site

To document a file available for downloading via **file transfer protocol**, provide the following information:

- author's name (if known)
- title of document, in quotation marks
- any print publication information, italicized or underlined where appropriate
- date of online publication (if known)
- date of access
- abbreviation *ftp*
- address of FTP site, with no closing punctuation
- full path to follow to find document

▶ Altar, Ted W. "Vitamin B12 and Vegans." 14 Jan.
     1993. 28 May 1996 ftp wiretap.spies.com
     Library/Article/Food/b12.txt.

You can use a URL (enclosed in angle brackets) instead of the command, address, and path elements.

▶ Fukuyama, Francis. "Immigrants and Family
     Values." <u>Commentary</u> May 1993. 19 Nov.
     1997 <ftp://heather.cs.ucdavis.edu/pub
     /Immigration/Index.html>.

▶ United States. Cong. Senate. <u>Safe and Afford-
     able Schools Act of 1997</u>. <u>Cong. Rec</u>. 21
     Jan. 1997. 20 Oct. 1997 <ftp://ftp.loc.gov
     /pub/thomas/c105/s1.is.txt>.

9 Gopher site

To document information obtained by using the **gopher** search protocol, provide the following information:

- author's name (if known)
- title of document, in quotation marks
- any print publication information, italicized or underlined where appropriate
- date of online publication (if known)

- date of access
- URL, in angle brackets

▶ Smith, Charles A. "National Extension Model of
      Critical Parenting Practices." 1994. 28
      May 1996 <gopher://tinman.mes.umn.edu:4242
      /11/Other/Other/NEM_Parent>.

To document the location of information using a gopher
command-path format, give the following information
instead of the URL:

- word *gopher*
- site name
- path followed to access document, with slashes to
  indicate menu selections

▶ Association for Progressive Communications.
      "About the APC." March 1997. 11 Dec. 1997
      gopher gopher.humanrights.org About IGC
      Networks/Association for Progressive
      Communications/About the APC.

10 Linkage data

To document a specific file (or information appearing in
a **frame** within a larger Web document) and give **linkage
data** showing its hypertext context, provide the following information:

- author's name (if known)
- title of document, in quotation marks
- abbreviation *lkd.* ("linked from")
- title of document to which file is linked, in italics or
  underlined
- additional linkage details (if applicable), preceded by
  at
- date of publication (if known)
- date of access
- URL for source document, in angle brackets

▶ Miller, Allison. "Allison Miller's Home Page."
      Lkd. <u>EKU Honors Program Home Page</u>, at
      "Personal Pages." N.d. 2 Apr. 1996 <http://
      www.csc.eku.edu/honors>.

► Teague, Jason Cranford. "Frames in Action."
        Lkd. <u>Kairos: A Journal for Teachers of
        Writing in Webbed Environments</u> 2.1 (1997)
        at "Cover Web: Tenure and Technology." 19
        Nov. 1997 <http://english.ttu.edu/kairos
        /2.1>.

Works Cited

Gibaldi, Joseph. *MLA Handbook for Writers of Research Papers.*
    New York: Modern Language Association of America,
    1995.
Modern Language Association. "Citing Sources from the
    World Wide Web." Lkd. *MLA on the Web* at "MLA Style."
    25 Nov. 1997. 26 Nov. 1997 <http://www.mla.org
    /main_stl.htm#sources>.

CHAPTER SIX

Using APA Style to Cite and Document Sources

The fourth edition of the *Publication Manual of the American Psychological Association* (1994) provides documentation advice for writers in the social sciences. Written primarily for authors preparing manuscripts for professional publication in scholarly journals, the manual discusses manuscript content and organization, writing style, and manuscript preparation. It also offers advice for student writers in an appendix.

The *Publication Manual* instructs writers to document quotations, paraphrases, summaries, and other information from sources as follows: "Document your study throughout the text by citing by author and date the works you researched. This style of citation briefly identifies the source for readers and enables them to locate the source of information in the alphabetical reference list at the end of an article" (p. 168). When using APA style, consult the *Publication Manual* for general style requirements (e.g., style for metric units) and for advice on preparing manuscripts and electronic texts. This chapter follows the conventions of APA citation style.

6a Adapting APA style to cite Internet sources

Although the *Publication Manual* gives recommendations for citing some kinds of electronic sources (e.g., subscriber-based and general-access online journal articles available via **email** or **FTP**), it acknowledges that "at the time of writing this edition, a standard had not yet emerged for referencing on-line information" (p. 218). Because the manual was published before the development of the **Internet** as we now know it, it does not have guidelines for citing **World Wide Web** sites, **Web discussion forum** postings, and other Internet sources. The following citation guidelines extend the principles and conventions of APA citation style to Internet sources.[1]

1 Link an in-text citation of an Internet source to a corresponding entry in the References.

In APA style, each text reference is linked to a specific entry in the list of References. The essential elements of an in-text citation are the author's last name (or the document's title, if no author is identified) and the date of publication. Information such as a page or chapter number

---

Box 6.1
Using italics and underlining in APA style

APA style italicizes certain elements (e.g., book and journal titles) in printed publications but recommends underlining those elements in manuscripts. The use of underlining to represent italics becomes a problem when you compose texts for online publication. On the World Wide Web, underlining in a document indicates that the underlined word or phrase is an active hypertext link. (All HTML editing programs automatically underline any text linked to another hypertext or Web site.)

When composing Web documents, avoid underlining. Instead, use italics for titles, for emphasis, and for words, letters, and numbers referred to as such. When you write with programs such as email that don't allow italics, type an underscore mark _like this_ before and after text you would otherwise italicize or underline.

---

[1]For final copy, the *Publication Manual* specifies the "hanging indent" format for references, with each entry's first line set flush left and subsequent lines indented. Unless your instructor suggests otherwise, it is the format we recommend. Note, however, that for manuscripts being submitted to journals, APA requires the reverse (first lines indented, subsequent lines set flush left), assuming that it will be converted by a typesetting system to a hanging indent.

may be added to show where in a source cited material appears.

Create an in-text reference to an Internet source by using a signal phrase, a parenthetical citation, or both a previewing sentence and a parenthetical citation.

Using a signal phrase To introduce a short quotation, paraphrase, or summary, mention the author's name either in an introductory signal phrase or in a parenthetical reference immediately following the signal phrase and containing the publication date. (See 4e for a discussion of signal phrases and verbs.)

> **signal phrase**

▶ Weisenmiller (1995) reported that "the Macintosh PowerPC has made a significant impact on the prepress industry of the southeastern United States" (Abstract).

> **signal phrase**

▶ According to one study (Weisenmiller, 1995), a majority of companies have adopted the Macintosh PowerPC into their company's produc- tion processes. Investment in Macintosh PowerPCs has generally created new workstations for these companies rather than replacing older workstations (chap. 5).

Here is the References entry for this source:

▶ Weisenmiller, E. M. (1995). The impact of the Macintosh PowerPC on the prepress industry of the southeastern United States. <http://teched.vt.edu/ElectronicPortfolios /Weisenmiller.ep/Thesistoc.html> (1996, May 26).

Using a parenthetical citation after cited material Place the author's name and the source's date of publication in parentheses immediately after the end of the cited material.

▶ Many companies have been successful in using the Macintosh PowerPC in the prepress process (Weisenmiller, 1995, chap. 5).

Using a previewing sentence and a parenthetical citation
To introduce and identify the source of a long quotation
(one comprising 40 or more words), use a previewing
sentence that names the author and ends in a colon. By
briefly announcing the content of an extended quotation, a previewing sentence tells readers what to look for
in the quotation. Indent the block quotation five spaces
(or one paragraph indent). At the end of the quotation,
after the final punctuation mark, indicate in parentheses
any text division that indicates the quotation's location
in the source document.

▶ The Librarians Association of the University of
  Chicago (1996) noted that recent developments
  in scholarly Internet publication now urge us
  to rethink the way we give credit to our
  sources:

> The ease with which authors can broadcast
> works worldwide through the new media
> makes understanding of copyright and fair
> use increasingly important. The ease of
> making digital recordings and of download-
> ing works from the Internet does not nec-
> essarily mean that the information can be
> adapted or reproduced without permission
> or royalty payment. Likewise, the lack of
> a copyright statement does not imply that
> a work is in the public domain. To avoid
> infringement of intellectual property
> rights, educators and students must exer-
> cise caution in producing their own educa-
> tional multimedia programs--especially if
> these are later published on the World-
> Wide Web. (II.A. Introduction)

Here is the References entry:

▶ Librarians Association of the University of
      California. (1996, February 1). New hori-
      zons in scholarly communication: Part 2.
      New publishing models. <http://www.ucsc
      .edu/scomm/publishing.html> (1996, May
      28).

2 Substitute Internet text divisions for page numbers.

The *Publication Manual* (1994) requires that "[you] give the author, year, and page number in parentheses (paragraph numbers may be used in place of page numbers for electronic text)" when you use a direct quotation (p. 97). Because Internet sources are rarely marked with page numbers, you will not always be able to show exactly where cited material comes from. If a source has internal divisions, use these instead of page numbers in your citation. Be sure to use divisions inherent in the document and not those provided by your browsing software.

▶ J. McGann (1996, May 6) pointed out that even
  decentered hypertexts are nevertheless always
  ordered: "To say that a HyperText is not cen-
  trally organized does not mean--at least does
  not mean to me--that the HyperText structure has
  no governing order(s), even at a theoretical
  level" (Coda: A Note on the Decentered Text).

Here is the References entry:

    McGann, J. (1996, May 6). The rationale of
        HyperText. <http://jefferson.village.vir
        ginia.edu/public/jjm2f/rationale.html>
        (1996, May 27).

3 Use source-reflective statements to show where cited material ends.

Many Internet sources appear as single screens. To let your readers know where your use of a single-screen Internet source with no text divisions ends, use a source-reflective statement.

Source-reflective statements give you an opportunity to assert your authorial voice. Writers use source-reflective statements to provide editorial comment, clarification, qualification, amplification, dissent, agreement, and so on. In the following example, the absence of a source-reflective statement creates uncertainty as to whether the writer has finished citing an Internet source or has merely moved from quoting directly to paraphrasing.

▶ Mike Sosteric observed that "in recent years, scholarly communication has virtually exploded into the on-line electronic world [and] this has brought a number of demonstrable benefits to the scholarly communication process." We can expect many more electronic journals to appear online in the next few years--surely a benefit to scholarly communications.

In the next example, the writer has added a source-reflective statement to show that use of the source has ended.

▶ Mike Sosteric observed that "in recent years, scholarly communication has virtually exploded into the on-line electronic world [and] this has brought a number of demonstrable benefits to the scholarly communication process."
 ⌐ Sosteric's observation means that we can expect many more electronic journals to appear online in the next few years--surely a benefit to scholarly communications.

 └──────── **source-reflective statement**

Here is the References entry:

▶ Sosteric, M. (1996). Electronic journals and scholarly communication: Notes and issues. <u>Electronic Journal of Sociology.</u> <http://129.128.113.200:8010/vol002.001/Sosteric-Abstract.html> (1996, October 21).

6b References

When using APA style, place a list of cited sources, arranged alphabetically, after the text of your essay but before any appendixes or explanatory notes. The *Publication Manual* (1994) gives the following general models for References entries:

Book

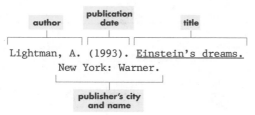

Lightman, A. (1993). <u>Einstein's dreams.</u>
New York: Warner.

Periodical article

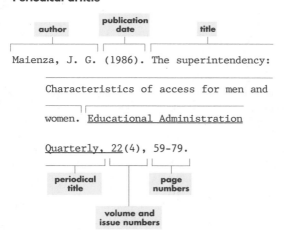

Maienza, J. G. (1986). The superintendency:

Characteristics of access for men and

women. <u>Educational Administration</u>

<u>Quarterly, 22</u>(4), 59-79.

The *Publication Manual* also presents numerous variations that accommodate a variety of print sources (e.g., translations, government documents). For detailed information on creating a References list, see Chapter 3 of the *Publication Manual*, "APA Editorial Style."

Extending the citation practice of the *Publication Manual* to include Internet sources produces the following model:

Online document

▶ Author's name (last name, first and any middle
      initials). (Date of Internet publication).
      Document title. <URL> or other retrieval
      information (Date of access).

Box 6.2
Using hypertext to document sources on the Web

The hypertext environment of the World Wide Web doesn't just alter the way you do research, it also lets you document sources in a new way—by using hypertext links. Electronic journals published on the Web are already replacing traditional notes, References listings, appendixes, and other supporting text with links to the documents being cited. To read more about hypertext documentation, see Chapter 10 in this book. For an example of how it works, look at articles published in the *Electronic Journal of Sociology* at <http://www.sociology.org>.

Internet sources differ in the kinds of information that are important for retrieval, and the model for each type of source reflects the information needed to retrieve that source. For example, for documents that originated as electronic mail (including personal email, newsgroup and HyperNews postings, and listserv messages), the author's email address is included after the author's name to help readers authenticate the source. The following models enable you to document Internet sources in a manner consistent with the principles of APA style.[2]

1 World Wide Web site

To document a file available for viewing and downloading via the **World Wide Web**, provide the following information:

- author's name (if known)
- date of publication or last revision (if known), in parentheses
- title of document
- title of complete work (if applicable), underlined
- URL, in angle brackets
- date of access, in parentheses

---

[2]These documentation models are much more compact than those suggested by others (Land, 1995; Li & Crane, 1993, 1996). The preliminary models in the *Publication Manual,* drawn from Li and Crane (1993), include descriptive expressions such as "[On-line]," "Available:," and "Hostname:," which are not necessary for understanding Internet specifications and also place potentially misleading symbols near electronic addresses.

Personal site

▶ Pellegrino, J. (1997, September 24). Homepage. <http://www.english.eku.edu/PELLEGRI /personal.htm> (1997, November 12).

General Web site

▶ Harris, J. G. (1997, April 19). The return of the witch hunts. <u>Witchhunt Information Page.</u> <http://liquid2-sun.mit.edu/fells .short.html> (1997, November 19).

▶ Shade, L. R. (1994, February 14). Gender issues in computer networking. <http://www.mit.edu :8001/people/sorokin/women/lrs.html> (1997, November 26).

Book

▶ Darwin, C. (1845; 1997, June). <u>The voyage of the</u> Beagle. Project Gutenberg. <ftp://uiarchive.cso.uiuc.edu/pub/etext /gutenberg/etext97/vbgle10.txt> (1997, October 1).

Article in an electronic journal (ejournal)

▶ Browning, T. (1997). Embedded visuals: Student design in Web spaces. <u>Kairos: A Journal for Teachers of Writing in Webbed Environments, 3</u>(1). <http://www.as.ttu.edu /kairos/2.1/features/browning/index.html> (1997, October 21).

Article in an electronic magazine (ezine)

▶ Myhrvold, N. (1997, June 12). Confessions of a cybershaman. <u>Slate.</u> <http://www.slate.com /CriticalMass/97-06-12/CriticalMass.asp> (1997, October 19).

Government publication

▶ Bush, G. (1989, April 12). Principles of ethical conduct for government officers and employees. Exec. Order No. 12674. Pt. 1. <http://www.usoge.gov/exorders/eo12674 .html> (1997, November 18).

To cite information appearing in a **frame** within a larger Web document, use the guidelines in 6b-10 for **linkage data**.

2 Email message

The *Publication Manual* categorizes all **electronic mail** as a form of personal communication that does not provide "recoverable data." The *Manual* advises against including personal communications in the References and suggests citing them only in the text. Many writers, however, consider it good practice to list email messages in the References, especially when a message's content is scholarly.

To document an email message, provide the following information:

- author's name (if known)
- author's email address, in angle brackets
- date of publication, in parentheses
- subject line from posting
- type of communication (personal email, distribution list, office communication), in square brackets
- date of access, in parentheses

▶ Franke, N. <frankel@llnl.gov> (1996, April 29). SoundApp 2.0.2 [Personal email]. (1996, May 3).

▶ Robinette, D. <robinetted@ccmail.gate.eku.edu> (1996, April 30). Epiphany project [Office communication]. (1996, May 23).

3 Web discussion forum posting

To document a posting to a **Web discussion forum**, provide the following information:

- author's name
- author's email address, in angle brackets
- date of publication, in parentheses
- subject line or title of posting
- type of message (if appropriate), in square brackets
- URL, in angle brackets
- date of access, in parentheses

▶ LaLiberte, D. <liberte@ncsa.uiuc.edu> (1996, May 23). HyperNews instructions. <http://union

.ncsa.uiuc.edu/HyperNews/get/hypernews
/instructions.html> (1996, May 24).

▶ Saffran, A. <saffran@wisbar.org> (1996, January
   5). It's not that hard [Reply to HyperNews
   instructions, by D. LaLiberte]. <http://
   union.ncsa.uiuc.edu/HyperNews/get/hypernews
   /instructions/90/1/1.html> (1996, May 24).

4 Listserv message

To document a **listserv** message, provide the following
information:

- author's name (if known)
- author's email address, in angle brackets
- date of publication, in parentheses
- subject line from posting
- address of listserv, in angle brackets
- date of access, in parentheses

▶ Parente, V. <vrparent@mailbox.syr.edu> (1996,
   May 27). On expectations of class partici-
   pation. <philosed@sued.syr.edu> (1996,
   May 29).

To document a file that can be retrieved from a list's
server or Web address, provide the following information after the subject line:

- address of listserv, in angle brackets
- address or URL for list's archive, preceded by *via* and
  enclosed in angle brackets
- date of access, in parentheses

▶ Carbone, N. <nickc@english.umass.edu> (1996,
   January 26). NN 960126: Followup to Don's
   comments about citing URLs. <acw-l@uni
   corn.acs.ttu.edu> via <http://www.ttu
   .edu/lists/acw-l> (1996, February 17).

5 Newsgroup message

To document information posted in a **newsgroup** discussion, provide the following information:

- author's name (if known)
- author's email address, in angle brackets
- date of publication, in parentheses
- subject line from posting
- name of newsgroup, in angle brackets
- date of access, in parentheses

▶ Slade, R. <res@maths.bath.ac.uk> (1996, March
    26). UNIX made easy. <alt.books.reviews>
    (1996, March 31).

If, after following all the suggestions in 4c-3, you cannot
determine the author's name, then use the author's
email address, enclosed in angle brackets, as the main
entry. When you alphabetize such sources in your
References, treat the first letter of the email address as
though it were capitalized.

▶ <lrm583@aol.com> (1996, May 26). Thinking of
    adoption. <alt.adoption> (1996, May 29).

6 Real-time communication

To document a **real-time communication**, such as those
posted in **MOOs**, **MUDs**, and **IRCs**, provide the following information:

- name of speaker(s) (if known), or name of site
- date of event, in parentheses
- title of event (if appropriate)
- type of communication (group discussion, personal
  interview), if not indicated elsewhere in entry, in
  square brackets
- address, using a URL (in angle brackets) or command-line directions
- date of access, in parentheses

▶ LambdaMOO. (1996, May 28). Seminar discussion
    on netiquette. <telnet://lambda.parc
    .xerox.edu:8888> (1996, May 28).

▶ Harnack, A. (1996, April 4). Words. [Group
    discussion]. telnet moo.du.org/port=8888
    (1996, April 5).

7 Telnet site

To document a **telnet** site or a file available via telnet, provide the following information:

- author's name (if known)
- date of publication (if known), in parentheses
- title of document (if known)
- title of full work (if applicable), underlined
- word *telnet*
- complete telnet address, with no closing punctuation
- directions for accessing document
- date of access, in parentheses

▶ Aquatic Conservation Network. (n.d.). About the
    Aquatic Conservation Network. <u>National
    Capital Freenet.</u> telnet freenet.carleton
    .ca login as guest, go acn, press 1
    (1996, May 28).

▶ California Department of Pesticide Regulation.
    (n.d.). Pest management information. <u>CSU
    Fresno ATI-NET.</u> telnet caticsuf.csufres
    no.edu login as super, press a, press k
    (1996, May 28).

8 FTP site

To document a file available for downloading via **file transfer protocol**, provide the following information:

- author's name (if known)
- date of publication (if known), in parentheses
- title of document
- any print publication information, underlined where appropriate
- abbreviation *ftp*
- address of FTP site, with no closing punctuation
- full path to follow to find document, with no closing punctuation
- date of access, in parentheses

▶ Altar, T. W. (1993, January 14). Vitamin B12 and
    vegans. ftp wiretap.spies.com Library
    /Article/Food/b12.txt (1996, May 28).

You can use a URL (enclosed in angle brackets) instead
of the command, address, and path elements.

▶ Fukuyama, F. (1993, May). Immigrants and family
      values. <ftp://heather.cs.ucdavis.edu/pub
      /Immigration/Index.html> (1997, November
      19).

▶ U.S. Senate. (1997, January 21). Safe and
      Affordable Schools Act of 1997. <u>Cong. Rec.</u>
      <ftp://ftp.loc.gov/pub/thomas/c105/s1.is
      .txt> (1997, October 21).

9 Gopher site

To document information obtained by using the **gopher**
search protocol, provide the following information:

- author's name (if known)
- date of online publication (if known), in parentheses
- title of document
- any print publication information, underlined where
  appropriate
- URL, in angle brackets
- date of access, in parentheses

▶ Smith, C. A. (1994). National extension model
      of critical parenting practices. <gopher://
      tinman.mes.umn.edu:4242/11/Other/Other
      /NEM_Parent> (1996, May 28).

To document the location of information using a gopher
command-path format, give the following information
instead of the URL:

- word *gopher*
- site name
- path followed to access document, with slashes to
  indicate menu selections

▶ Association for Progressive Communications.
      (1997, March). About the APC. gopher
      gopher/humanrights.org About IGC
      Networks/Association for Progressive
      Communications/About the APC (1997,
      December 11).

10 Linkage data

To document a specific file (or information appearing in a **frame** within a larger document) and give **linkage data** showing its hypertext context, provide the following information:

- author's name (if known)
- date of publication (if known), in parentheses
- title of document
- abbreviation *lkd.* ("linked from")
- title of document to which file is linked, underlined
- additional linkage details (if applicable), preceded by *at*
- URL for source document, in angle brackets
- date of access, in parentheses

▶ Miller, A. (n.d.). Allison Miller's home page. Lkd. <u>EKU Honors Program Home Page,</u> at "Personal Pages." <http://www.csc.eku .edu/honors> (1996, April 2).

▶ Teague, J. C. (1997, March 11). Frames in action. Lkd. <u>Kairos: A Journal for Teachers of Writing in Webbed Environments</u> at "Cover Web: Tenure and Technology." <http://english.ttu.edu/kairos/2.1> (1997, November 19).

Reference

American Psychological Association. (1994). *Publication Manual of the American Psychological Association* (4th ed.). Washington, DC: American Psychological Association.

CHAPTER SEVEN

Using *Chicago* Style to Cite and Document Sources

This chapter's guidelines for citing Internet sources are based on the principles presented in the fourteenth edition of *The Chicago Manual of Style*.[1] The *Chicago Manual* offers two documentation styles, one using notes and bibliographies, the other using author-date citations and lists of references. The *Chicago Manual* also gives guidelines for spelling and punctuation and discusses the treatment of numbers, quotations, illustrations, tables, foreign languages, mathematical symbols, abbreviations, and so on.

To mark citations in the text, the *Chicago Manual*'s note-bibliography style places a superscript number after each quotation, paraphrase, or summary. Citations are numbered sequentially throughout the text, and each citation corresponds to a numbered note containing publication information about the source cited. Such notes are called *footnotes* when printed at the foot of a page and *endnotes* when printed at the end of an essay, chapter, or book. These notes generally serve two purposes: to cite sources and to make cross-references to previous notes. This chapter follows the conventions of the *Chicago Manual*'s note-bibliography style.

---

[1]*The Chicago Manual of Style,* 14th ed. (Chicago: University of Chicago Press, 1993). When this chapter cites the *Chicago Manual,* it does so in footnotes such as this one.

7a Adapting *Chicago* style to cite Internet sources

Although the *Chicago Manual* provides some advice for documenting information from computerized data services, computer programs, and electronic documents, it contains no advice on documenting Internet sources. The following recommendations adapt the *Chicago Manual*'s guidelines and models to Internet sources.

1 Introduce the source of a short quotation, paraphrase, or summary by using either a signal phrase set off by a comma or a signal verb with a *that* clause.

The following two examples show how signal phrases can be used to introduce cited material. (See 4e for a discussion of signal phrases and verbs.)

signal phrase

▶ According to Brendan P. Kehoe, "We are truly in an information society. Now more than ever, moving vast amounts of information quickly across great distances is one of our most pressing needs."[1]

signal phrase

▶ Brendan P. Kehoe reminds us that "we are truly in an information society. Now more than ever, moving vast amounts of information quickly across great distances is one of our most pressing needs."[1]

Here is the note for this source:

▶   1. Brendan P. Kehoe, <u>Zen and the Art of the Internet,</u> January 1992, <http://freenet.buffa lo.edu/~popmusic/zen10.txt> (4 June 1996), Network Basics.

> **Box 7.1**
> **Using italics and underlining in *Chicago* style**
>
> *Chicago* style recommends italicizing certain elements (e.g., book and journal titles) in printed text. Use underlining if your instructor requires it or if your typewriter or wordprocessing program can't produce italics. However, the use of underlining to represent italics becomes a problem when you compose texts for online publication. On the World Wide Web, underlining in a document indicates that the underlined word or phrase is an active hypertext link. (All HTML editing programs automatically underline any text linked to another hypertext or Web site.)
>
> When composing Web documents, avoid underlining. Instead, use italics for titles, for emphasis, and for words, letters, and numbers referred to as such. When you write with programs such as email that don't allow italics, type an underscore mark _like this_ before and after text you would otherwise italicize or underline.

2 Link an in-text citation of an Internet source to a corresponding note.

According to *Chicago* style, the first note for a given source should include all the information necessary to identify and locate the source: the author's full name, the full title of the book, the name of the editor, the place of publication, the name of the publisher, the publication date, and page numbers indicating the location of the quoted information. In subsequent references to the source, give only the author's last name followed by a comma, a shortened version of the title followed by a comma, and the page reference.

Indent the first line of each note five spaces (or one paragraph indent). Begin with a number followed by a period. Leave one space before the first word of the note. If you are double-spacing your manuscript, double-space the notes as well.

Book (first note)

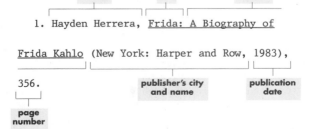

1. Hayden Herrera, <u>Frida: A Biography of Frida Kahlo</u> (New York: Harper and Row, 1983), 356.

author · title · subtitle · publisher's city and name · publication date · page number

Book (subsequent note)

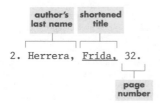

2. Herrera, <u>Frida,</u> 32.

Periodical article (first note)

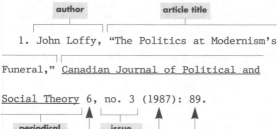

1. John Loffy, "The Politics at Modernism's

Funeral," <u>Canadian Journal of Political and</u>

<u>Social Theory</u> 6, no. 3 (1987): 89.

Periodical article (subsequent note)

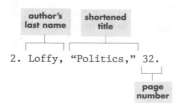

2. Loffy, "Politics," 32.

Here is how you would document the first reference to a source:

▶ According to Professor Tom Wilson, "the idea of the electronic library has emerged as a model for future systems, already implemented in some forms and to some degree in various places."[1]

Here is the corresponding note:

▶   1. Tom Wilson, "'In the Beginning Was the
Word': Social and Economic Factors in Scholarly
Electronic Communication," ELVIRA Conference
Keynote Paper, 1009, 10 April 1995, <http://
www2.shef.ac.uk/infor_studies/lecturer/elvira
.html> (23 May 1996), Introduction.

Here is a second reference to the source:

▶ Professor Wilson contends that "a new system of
scholarly communication, based on electronic
systems and networks, not only necessitates new
models for the concepts of journals, library,
and publishing, but also new interpersonal and
institutional mores, customs, and practices."[2]

Here is the note:

▶   2. Wilson, "'In the Beginning,'" Introduction.

3 Substitute Internet text divisions for page numbers.

The *Chicago Manual* requires that a note include a page
reference or similar information for locating material in a
source. Because Internet sources are rarely marked with
page numbers, you will not always be able to show exactly
where cited material comes from. If a source has internal
divisions, use these instead of page numbers in your citation. Be sure to use divisions inherent in the document
and not those provided by your browsing software.

In the following example, the Introduction serves as a
text division for an Internet source.

▶ As TyAnna Herrington observes, "Nicholas
Negroponte's <u>Being Digital</u> provides another welcome not only into an age of technological
ubiquity, but into a way of 'being' with technology."[1]

Here is the note:

▶   1. TyAnna K. Herrington, "Being Is
Believing," review of <u>Being Digital,</u> by
Nicholas Negroponte, <u>Kairos: A Journal for
Teaching Writing in Webbed Environments</u> 1.1

Box 7.2
Using hypertext to document sources on the Web

The hypertext environment of the World Wide Web doesn't just
alter the way you do research, it also lets you document sources
in a new way—by using hypertext links. Electronic journals published on the Web are already replacing traditional notes, bibliographies, appendixes, and other supporting text with links to the
documents being cited. To read more about hypertext documentation, see Chapter 10 in this book. For an example of how it
works, look at the format of the *Harvard Educational Review* at
<http://hugse1.harvard.edu/~hepg/her.html>.

(1996), <http://english.ttu.edu/kairos/1.1> (24
May 1996), Introduction.

7b Notes

See 7a-2 for the basic *Chicago*-style models for documenting printed books and periodicals. For additional information about documenting print sources, see Chapters 15
and 16 of the *Chicago Manual*.

Extending the citation practice of the *Chicago Manual*
to include Internet sources produces the following model:

▶   1. Author's name (in normal order), document
title, date of Internet publication, <URL> or
other retrieval information (date of access),
text division (if applicable).

This model combines the stylistic elements of *Chicago*-
style author-date citation[2] with the elements necessary for
identifying an Internet source. The publication date
appears close to the title of the document, while the date
of access follows the **URL** or other access information.
The text division occupies the final position in the note, as
page numbers would for a printed source.

Internet sources differ in the kinds of information that
are important for retrieval, and the model for each type of
source reflects the information needed to retrieve that
source. For example, for documents that originated as **electronic mail** (including personal email, **newsgroup** and
Web discussion forum postings, and **listserv** messages),
the author's email address is included after the author's
name to help readers authenticate the source. The follow-

---

[2]See *Chicago Manual,* sections 15.154 and 15.231.

ing models enable you to document Internet sources in a manner consistent with the principles of *Chicago* style.

1 World Wide Web site

To document a file available for viewing and download-ing via the **World Wide Web**, provide the following information:

- author's name (if known)
- title of document, in quotation marks
- title of complete work (if applicable), in italics or underlined
- date of publication or last revision (if known)
- URL, in angle brackets
- date of access, in parentheses

Personal site

▶   1. Joseph Pellegrino, "Homepage," 24 September 1997, <http://www.english.eku.edu /pellegri/personal.htm> (7 November 1997).

General Web site

▶   1. Jonathan G. Harris, "The Return of the Witch Hunts," <u>Witchhunt Information Page,</u> 19 April 1997, <http://liquid2-sun.mit.edu/fells .short.html> (19 November 1997).

▶   2. Leslie R. Shade, "Gender Issues in Computer Networking," 14 February 1994, <http://www.mit.edu:8001/people/sorokin/women /lrs.html> (26 November 1997).

Book

▶   1. Charles Darwin, <u>The Voyage of the</u> Beagle (London, 1845), Project Gutenberg, June 1997, <ftp://uiarchive.cso.uiuc.edu/pub/etext /gutenberg/etext97/vbgle10.txt> (1 October 1997).

Article in an electronic journal (ejournal)

▶   1. Tonya Browning, "Embedded Visuals: Student Design in Web Spaces," <u>Kairos: A Journal for Teachers of Writing in Webbed Environments</u> 3, no. 1 (1997) <http://english.ttu.edu/kairos

/2.1/features/browning/index.html> (21 October
1997).

Article in an electronic magazine (ezine)

▶   1. Nathan Myhrvold, "Confessions of a
Cybershaman," <u>Slate,</u> 12 June 1997, <http://www
.slate.com/CriticalMass/97-06-12/CriticalMass
.asp> (19 October 1997).

Government publication

▶   1. George Bush, "Principles of Ethical
Conduct for Government Officers and Employees,"
Executive Order 12674, 12 April 1989, pt. 1,
<http://www.usoge.gov/exorders/eo12674.html>
(30 October 1997).

To cite information appearing in a **frame** within a larger
Web document, use the guidelines in 7b-10 for **linkage
data**.

2 Email message

To document an **email** message, provide the following
information:

- author's name (if known)
- author's email address, in angle brackets
- subject line from posting, in quotation marks
- date of publication
- type of communication (personal email, distribution
  list, office communication)
- date of access, in parentheses

▶   1. Norman Franke, <frankel@llnl.gov>
"SoundApp 2.0.2," 29 April 1996, personal email
(3 May 1996).

▶   2. Danny Robinette, <robinetted@ccmail
.gate.eku.edu> "Epiphany Project," 30 April
1996, office communication (29 May 1996).

3 Web discussion forum posting

To document a posting to a **Web discussion forum**, provide the following information:

- author's name
- author's email address, in angle brackets
- subject line or title of posting, in quotation marks
- date of publication
- type of message (if appropriate)
- URL, in angle brackets
- date of access, in parentheses

▶ 1. Daniel LaLiberte, <liberte@ncsa.uiuc.edu>
"HyperNews Instructions," 23 May 1996, <http://
union.ncsa.uiuc.edu/HyperNews/get/hypernews
/instructions.html> (24 May 1996).

▶ 2. Art Saffran, <saffran@wisbar.org> "It's
Not That Hard," 5 January 1996, reply to
"HyperNews Instructions" by Daniel LaLiberte,
<http://union.ncsa.uiuc.edu/HyperNews/get
/hypernews/instructions/90/1/1.html> (24 May
1996).

4 Listserv message

To document a **listserv** message, provide the following
information:

- author's name (if known)
- author's email address, in angle brackets
- subject line from posting, in quotation marks
- date of publication
- address of listserv, in angle brackets
- date of access, in parentheses

▶ 1. Victor Parente, <vrparent@mailbox.syr.edu>
"On Expectations of Class Participation," 27
May 1996, <philosed@sued.syr.edu> (29 May 1996).

To document a file that can be retrieved from a list's
server or Web address, provide the following information
after the publication date:

- address of listserv, in angle brackets
- address or URL for list's archive, preceded by *via* and
  enclosed in angle brackets
- date of access, in parentheses

▶ 1. Nick Carbone, <nickc@english.umass.edu>
"NN 960126: Followup to Don's Comments about
Citing URLs," 26 January 1996, <acw-l@unicorn
.acs.ttu.edu> via <http://www.ttu.edu/lists
/acw-l> (17 February 1996).

5 Newsgroup message

To document information posted in a **newsgroup** discussion, provide the following information:

- author's name (if known)
- author's email address, in angle brackets
- subject line from posting, in quotation marks
- date of publication
- name of newsgroup, in angle brackets
- date of access, in parentheses

▶ 1. Robert Slade, <res@maths.bath.ac.uk> "UNIX
Made Easy," 26 March 1996, <alt.books.reviews>
(31 March 1996).

If, after following all the suggestions in 4c-3, you cannot
determine the author's name, then use the author's email
address, enclosed in angle brackets, as the main entry.
When you alphabetize such sources in your Bibliography,
treat the first letter of the email address as though it were
capitalized.

▶ 2. <lrm583@aol.com> "Thinking of Adoption,"
26 May 1996, <alt.adoption> (29 May 1996).

6 Real-time communication

To document a **real-time communication**, such as those
posted in **MOOs**, **MUDs**, and **IRCs**, provide the following information:

- name of speaker(s) (if known), or name of site
- title of event (if appropriate), in quotation marks
- date of event
- type of communication (group discussion, personal interview), if not indicated elsewhere in entry
- address, using a URL (in angle brackets) or command-line directions

- date of access, in parentheses

▶   1. LambdaMOO, "Seminar Discussion on Netiquette," 28 May 1996, <telnet://lambda.parc .xerox.edu:8888> (28 May 1996).

▶   2. Andrew Harnack, "Words," 4 April 1996, group discussion, telnet moo.du.org/port=8888 (5 April 1996).

7 Telnet site

To document a **telnet** site or a file available via telnet, provide the following information:

- author's name (if known)
- title of document (if known), in quotation marks
- title of full work (if applicable), in italics or underlined
- date of publication (if known)
- word *telnet*
- complete telnet address, with no closing punctuation
- directions for accessing document
- date of access, in parentheses

▶   1. Aquatic Conservation Network, "About the Aquatic Conservation Network," National Capital Freenet, n.d., telnet freenet.carleton.ca login as guest, go acn, press 1 (28 May 1996).

▶   2. California Department of Pesticide Regulation, "Pest Management Information," CSU Fresno ATI-NET, n.d., telnet caticsuf.csufres no.edu login as super, press a, press k (28 May 1996).

8 FTP site

To document a file for downloading via **file transfer protocol**, provide the following information:

- author's name (if known)
- title of document, in quotation marks
- date of publication (if known)
- any print publication information, italicized or underlined where appropriate

- abbreviation *ftp*
- address of FTP site, with no closing punctuation
- full path to follow to find document, with no closing punctuation
- date of access, in parentheses

▶   1. Ted W. Altar, "Vitamin B12 and Vegans,"
14 January 1993, ftp wiretap.spies.com#Library
/Article/Food/b12.txt (28 May 1996).

You can use a URL (enclosed in angle brackets) instead of the command, address, and path elements.

▶   2. Francis Fukuyama, "Immigrants and Family
Values," May 1993, <ftp://heather.cs.ucdavis
.edu/pub/Immigration/Index.html> (19 November
1997).

▶   3. U.S. Senate, "Safe and Affordable Schools
Act of 1997," <u>Congressional Record</u>, 21 January
1997 <ftp://ftp.loc.gov/pub/thomas/c105/s1.is
.txt> (20 October 1997).

9 Gopher site

To document information obtained by using the **gopher** search protocol, provide the following information:

- author's name (if known)
- title of document, in quotation marks
- any print publication information, italicized or underlined where appropriate
- date of online publication (if known)
- URL, in angle brackets
- date of access, in parentheses

▶   1. Charles A. Smith, "National Extension
Model of Critical Parenting Practices," 1994,
<gopher://tinman.mes.umn.edu:4242/11/Other/Other
/NEM_Parent> (28 May 1996).

To document the location of information using a gopher command-path format, give the following information instead of the URL:

- word *gopher*
- site name

- path followed to access document, with slashes to indicate menu selections

▶ 2. Association for Progressive Communications, "About the APC," March 1997, gopher
gopher.humanrights.org About IGC Networks
/Association for Progressive Communications
/About the APC (11 December 1997).

10 Linkage data

To document a specific file (or information appearing in a
frame within a larger Web document) and give **linkage
data** showing its hypertext context, provide the following
information:

- author's name (if known)
- title of document, in quotation marks
- abbreviation *lkd.* ("linked from")
- title of document to which file is linked, in italics or underlined
- additional linkage information (if applicable), preceded by *at*
- date of publication (if known)
- URL for source document, in angle brackets
- date of access, in parentheses

▶ 1. Allison Miller, "Allison Miller's Home
Page," lkd. <u>EKU Honors Program Home Page,</u> at
"Personal Pages," n.d., <http://www.csc.eku.edu
/honors> (2 April 1996).

▶ 2. Jason Crawford Teague, "Frames in Action,"
lkd. <u>Kairos: A Journal for Teachers of Writing
in Webbed Environments</u> at "Cover Web: Tenure
and Technology," 11 March 1997, <http://english
.ttu.edu/kairos/2.1> (19 November 1997).

7c Bibliography

Since the first note reference to a source includes all the
information necessary to verify or retrieve a citation, your
Chicago-style research paper may not include a
Bibliography. If you decide to include one (or are required
to do so by an instructor or editor), an alphabetized list of

sources will do the trick. (The Bibliography may also be titled Sources Consulted, Works Cited, or Selected Bibliography, if any of those titles more accurately describes the list.)

Bibliography entries differ from first note references in the following ways:

1. Authors' names are inverted.
2. Elements of entries are separated by periods.
3. The first line of each entry is flush with the left margin, and subsequent lines are indented three or four spaces.

If the rest of your manuscript is typed double-spaced, double-space the Bibliography as well.

Compare the following note with the corresponding Bibliography entry:

▶   2. Jason Crawford Teague, "Frames in Action," lkd. <u>Kairos: A Journal for Teachers of Writing in Webbed Environments</u> at "Cover Web: Tenure and Technology," 11 March 1997, <http://english.ttu.edu/kairos/2.1> (19 November 1997).

▶ Teague, Jason Crawford. "Frames in Action." Lkd. <u>Kairos: A Journal for Teachers of Writing in Webbed Environments</u> at "Cover Web: Tenure and Technology." 11 March 1997. <http://english.ttu.edu/kairos/2.1> (19 November 1997).

CHAPTER EIGHT

Using CBE Style to Cite and Document Sources

This chapter's guidelines for citing Internet sources stem from the principles presented in the sixth edition of *Scientific Style and Format: The CBE Manual for Authors, Editors, and Publishers,* published by the Council of Biology Editors in 1994. Many writers in the natural sciences use the citation style recommended in the *CBE Manual,* which also gives advice for styling and formatting scientific papers, journals, and books for publication. Its editors offer two methods for citing and documenting sources: the citation-sequence system and the name-year system.

8a   Using CBE in-text citation style

This section briefly describes the citation-sequence and name-year citation systems. Use the system preferred by your instructor or by the journal you are writing for, and consult Chapter 30 of the *CBE Manual,* "Citations and References," for detailed advice. The **Internet** documentation models presented in 8b are compatible with the principles of both systems.

> **Box 8.1**
> **Using italics and underlining in CBE style**
>
> CBE style doesn't specify the use of italics or underlining in
> References entries, leaving such matters to the discretion of writers
> and editors. In your writing, you may decide that you need to
> highlight certain titles, terms, or symbols. The use of underlining to
> represent italics becomes a problem when you compose texts for
> online publication. On the World Wide Web, underlining in a
> document indicates that the underlined word or phrase is an
> active hypertext link. (All HTML editing programs automatically
> underline any text linked to another hypertext or Web site.)
>
> When composing Web documents, avoid underlining. Instead,
> use italics for titles, for emphasis, and for words, letters, and num-
> bers referred to as such. When you write with programs such as
> email that don't allow italics, type an underscore mark _like this_
> before and after text you would otherwise italicize or underline.

1 The citation-sequence system

When using the citation-sequence system, key cited
sources to a list of references that are numbered in the
order in which they appear in the text. Use a superscript
number[1] or a number in parentheses (1) following any
reference to a source. (Most instructors prefer superscript
numbers to numbers in parentheses. If you're a student,
ask your instructor which style he or she prefers.) If a single reference points to more than one source, list the
source numbers[1,3,6] in a series. Use a comma (but no following space) to separate two numbers, or numbers[1,3]
that do not form a sequence. Use a dash to separate more
than two numbers[1-3] that form a sequence. If you cite a
source again later in the paper, refer to it by its original
number.

In the citation-sequence format, the date of publication
is listed after the publisher's name (for books) or after the
periodical name (for articles). The following example
uses the citation-sequence system.

▶ Ungvarski[1] claims that most HIV-positive
patients lose weight as their illness progress-
es. The World Health Organization has recognized HIV wasting syndrome as an AIDS-defining
condition.[2]

> HIV wasting is caused partly by an increase in the level of tumor necrosis factor (TNF). . . . This increase in TNF leads to the accelerated muscle breakdown characteristic of HIV wasting syndrome.[1,3]

Here are the References entries for these three sources:

▶ [1]Ungvarski PJ, Staats J. HIV/AIDS: A guide to nursing care. 3rd ed. Philadelphia: WB Saunders; 1995. p 47.
[2]World Health Organization. World health statistics annual: 1993. Geneva: World Health Organization; 1994.
[3]Coodley GO, Loveless MO, Merrill TM. The HIV wasting syndrome: a review. J Acquired Immune Deficiency Syndromes 1994 July;7(7):681–94. p 681.

2 The name-year system

When using the name-year system, key cited sources to an alphabetically arranged list of references. In the name-year format, the date of publication immediately follows the author's name. The following example uses the name-year system.

▶ The discovery in normal cells of genes capable of causing tumors can be considered a milestone in cancer research (Stehelin and others 1976). Recent work (Sarkar, Zhao, and Sarkar 1995) has confirmed the importance of this finding. As Bishop and Varmus (1985) point out, numerous results now suggest that changes in these genes transform normal cells into cancerous ones.

Here are the References entries for these three sources:

▶ Bishop JM, Varmus HE. 1985. Functions and origins of retroviral transforming genes. In: Weiss R, Teich N, Varmus HE, Coffin J, editors. RNA tumor viruses. Cold Spring Harbor, NY: Cold Spring Harbor Laboratory Press. p 999–1019.

▶ Sarkar T, Zhao W, Sarkar NH. 1995 Oct.
Expression of jun oncogene in rodent
and human breast tumors. World Wide Web J
Biology 1(1). <http://www.epress.com
/w3jbio/wj6.html> Accessed 1996 23 Oct.

▶ Stehelin D, Varmus HE, Bishop JM, Vogt PK.
1976. DNA related to the transforming gene(s)
of avian sarcoma viruses is present in normal
avian DNA. Nature 260:170–73.

8b References

The *CBE Manual* provides models for documenting electronic journal articles and books, some of which are available on the World Wide Web and by FTP and gopher.
The Council of Biology Editors has established conventions for citing electronically published articles and
books, and you are encouraged to follow them as out-
lined in the *CBE Manual*. When you cite other Internet
sources, use the guidelines in this section. The examples
shown follow the citation-sequence system, but you can
easily adapt them to the name-year system by deleting
the superscripts and alphabetizing the entries.

List the References at the end of your research paper
but before any appendixes or explanatory notes. For
Internet sources, use the following model:

▶ Author's name (last name, first and any middle
initials). Date of Internet publication.
Document title. <URL> or other retrieval information. Date of access.

Box 8.2
Using hypertext to document sources on the Web

The hypertext environment of the World Wide Web doesn't just
alter the way you do research, it also lets you document sources
in a new way—by using hypertext links. Electronic journals published on the Web are already replacing traditional notes,
References listings, appendixes, and other supporting text with
links to the documents being cited. To read more about hypertext
documentation, see Chapter 10 in this book. For an example of
how it works, look at the format of *The World Wide Web Journal
of Biology* at <http://epress.com/w3jbio>.

Internet sources differ in the kinds of information that are important for retrieval, and the model for each type of source reflects the information needed to retrieve that source. For example, for documents that originated as **electronic mail** (including personal email, **newsgroup** and **Web discussion forum** postings, and **listserv** messages), the author's email address is included after the author's name to help readers authenticate the source. The following models enable you to document Internet sources in a manner consistent with the principles of CBE style.

1 World Wide Web site

To document a file available for viewing and downloading via the **World Wide Web**, provide the following information:

- author's name (if known)
- date of publication or last revision (if known)
- title of document
- title of complete work (if applicable)
- URL, in angle brackets
- date of access

Personal site

▶ [1]Pellegrino J. 1997 Sept 24. Homepage. <http://www.english.eku.edu/PELLEGRI/personal.htm> Accessed 1997 Nov 7.

General Web site

▶ [1]Tardent P. 1995 Nov. Cell biology, annual report 1994. <http://www.unizh.ch/~zool/depts/cell/report94.html> Accessed 1996 Jun 18.

Book

▶ [1]Darwin C. 1845; 1997 Jun. The voyage of the Beagle. Project Gutenberg. <ftp://uiarchive.cso.uiuc.edu/pub/etext/gutenberg/etext97/vbgle10.txt> Accessed 1997 Oct 1.

Article in an electronic journal (ejournal)

▶ [1]Browning T. 1997. Embedded visuals: student design in Web spaces. Kairos: A Journal for

Teachers of Writing in Webbed Environments
3(1). <http://www.as.ttu.edu/kairos/2.1/features
/browning/index.html> Accessed 1997 Oct 21.

Article in an electronic magazine (ezine)

▶ [1]Myhrvold N. 1997 Jun 12. Confessions of a
cybershaman. Slate. <http://www.slate.com
/CriticalMass/97-06-12/CriticalMass.asp>
Accessed 1997 Oct 19.

▶ [2]Glockle WG, Nonnenmacher TF. 1995. A fractional
calculus approach to self-similar protein
dynamics. Biophysical J Abstr 68(1):46. <http://
biosci.cbs.umn.edu/biophys/bj/df-html/df95
/jan95.html#NN> Accessed 1996 Jul 25.

Government publication

▶ [1]Bush G. 1989 Apr 12. Principles of ethical
conduct for government officers and employees.
Executive Order 12674. Part 1. <http://www.usoge
.gov/exorders/eo12674.html> Accessed 1997 Nov 18.

To cite information appearing in a **frame** within a larger
Web document, use the guidelines in 8b-10 for **linkage
data**.

2 Email message

To document an **email** message, provide the following
information:

- author's name (if known)
- author's email address, in angle brackets
- date of publication
- subject line from posting
- type of communication (personal email, distribution
  list, office communication), in square brackets
- date of access

▶ [1]Franke N. <frankel@llnl.gov> 1996 Apr 29.
SoundApp 2.0.2 [Personal email]. Accessed 1996
May 3.

▶ [2]Robinette D. <robinetted@ccmail.gate.eku.edu>
1996 Apr 30. Epiphany project [Office communi-
cation]. Accessed 1996 May 23.

3 Web discussion forum posting

To document a posting to a **Web discussion forum**, provide the following information:

- author's name
- author's email address, in angle brackets
- date of publication
- subject line or title of posting
- type of message (if appropriate), in square brackets
- URL, in angle brackets
- date of access

▶ ¹LaLiberte D. <liberte@ncsa.uiuc.edu> 1996 May 23. HyperNews instructions. <http://union.ncsa .uiuc.edu/HyperNews/get/hypernews/instructions .html> Accessed 1996 May 24.

▶ ²Saffran A. <saffran@wisbar.org> 1996 Jan 5. It's not that hard [Reply to HyperNews instruc- tions, by D. LaLiberte]. <http://union.ncsa.uiuc .edu/HyperNews/get/hypernews/instructions /90/1/1.html> Accessed 1996 May 24.

4 Listserv message

To document a **listserv** message, provide the following information:

- author's name (if known)
- author's email address, in angle brackets
- date of publication
- subject line from posting
- address of listserv, in angle brackets
- date of access

▶ ¹Parente V. <vrparent@mailbox.syr.edu> 1996 May 27. On expectations of class participation. <philosed@sued.syr.edu> Accessed 1996 May 29.

To document a file that can be retrieved from a list's server or Web address, provide the following information after the publication date:

- address of listserv, in angle brackets

- address or URL for list's archive, preceded by *via* and enclosed in angle brackets
- date of access

▶ ²Carbone N. <nickc@english.umass.edu> 1996 Jan 26. NN 960126: followup to Don's comments about citing URLs. <acw-l@unicorn.acs.ttu.edu> via <http://www.ttu.edu/lists/acw-l> Accessed 1996 Feb 17.

5 Newsgroup message

To document information posted in a **newsgroup** discussion, provide the following information:

- author's name (if known)
- author's email address, in angle brackets
- date of publication
- subject line from posting
- name of newsgroup, in angle brackets
- date of access

▶ ¹Slade R. <res@maths.bath.ac.uk> 1996 Mar 26. UNIX made easy. <alt.books.reviews> Accessed 1996 Mar 31.

If, after following all the suggestions in 4c-3, you cannot determine the author's name, then use the author's email address, enclosed in angle brackets, as the main entry.

▶ ²<lrm583@aol.com> 1996 May 26. Thinking of adoption. <alt.adoption> Accessed 1996 May 29.

6 Real-time communication

To document a **real-time communication**, such as those posted in **MOOs**, **MUDs**, and **IRCs**, provide the following information:

- name of speaker(s) (if known), or name of site
- date of event
- title of event (if appropriate)
- type of communication (group discussion, personal interview), if not indicated elsewhere in entry, in square brackets

- address, using a URL (in angle brackets) or command-line directions
- date of access

▶ [1]LambdaMOO. 1996 May 28. Seminar discussion on netiquette. <telnet://lambda.parc.xerox.edu :8888> Accessed 1996 May 28.

▶ [2]Harnack A. 1996 Apr 4. Words. [Group discussion]. telnet moo.du.org/port=8888 Accessed 1996 Apr 5.

7 Telnet site

To document a **telnet** site or a file available via telnet, provide the following information:

- author's name (if known)
- date of publication (if known)
- title of document
- title of full work (if applicable)
- word *telnet*
- complete telnet address, with no closing punctuation
- directions for accessing document
- date of access

▶ [1]Aquatic Conservation Network. n.d. About the Aquatic Conservation Network. National Capital Freenet. telnet freenet.carleton.ca login as guest, go acn, press 1 Accessed 1996 May 28.

▶ [2]California Department of Pesticide Regulation. n.d. Pest management information. CSU Fresno ATI-NET. telnet caticsuf.csufresno.edu login as super, press a, press k Accessed 1996 May 28.

8 FTP site

To document a file available for downloading via **file transfer protocol**, provide the following information:

- author's name (if known)
- date of publication (if known)
- title of document
- any print publication information
- abbreviation *ftp*

- address of FTP site, with no closing punctuation
- full path to follow to find document, with no closing punctuation
- date of access

▶ [1]Altar TW. 1993 Jan 14. Vitamin B12 and vegans. ftp wiretap.spies.com Library/Article/Food /b12.txt Accessed 1996 May 28.

You can use a URL (enclosed in angle brackets) instead of the command, address, and path elements.

▶ [2]Fukuyama F. 1993 May. Immigrants and family values. <ftp://heather.cs.ucdavis.edu/pub /Immigration/Index.html> Accessed 1997 Nov 19.

▶ [3]Senate (US). 1997 Jan 21. Safe and Affordable Schools Act of 1997. Congressional Record. <ftp://ftp.loc.gov/pub/thomas/c105/s1.is.txt> Accessed 1997 Oct 20.

9 Gopher site

To document information obtained by using the **gopher** search protocol, provide the following information:

- author's name (if known)
- date of online publication (if known)
- title of document
- any print publication information
- URL, in angle brackets
- date of access

▶ [1]Smith CA. 1994. National extension model of critical parenting practices. <gopher://tinman .mes.umn.edu:4242/11/Other/Other/NEM_Parent> Accessed 1996 May 28.

To document the location of information using a gopher command-path format, give the following information instead of the URL:

- word *gopher*
- site name
- path followed to access document, with slashes to indicate menu selections

▶ ²Association for Progressive Communications.
1997 Mar. About the APC. gopher gopher
.humanrights.org About the IGC Networks
/Association for Progressive Communications
/About the APC Accessed 1997 Dec 11.

10 Linkage data

To document a specific file (or information appearing in a
frame within a larger Web document) and give **linkage
data** showing its hypertext context, provide the following
information:

- author's name (if known)
- date of publication (if known)
- title of document
- abbreviation *lkd.* ("linked from")
- title of document to which file is linked
- additional linkage details (if applicable), preceded by
  at
- URL for source document, in angle brackets
- date of access

▶ ¹Miller A. n.d. Allison Miller's home page. Lkd.
EKU honors program home page, at Personal
pages. <http://www.csc.eku.edu/honors> Accessed
1996 Apr 2.

▶ ²Teague JC. 1997 Mar 11. Frames in action. Lkd.
Kairos: A Journal for Teachers of Writing in
Webbed Environments, at Cover Web: Tenure and
Technology. <http://english.ttu.edu/kairos/2.1
.html> Accessed 1997 Nov 19.

CHAPTER NINE

Observing Netiquette

Netiquette (a combination of the words *net* and *etiquette*) refers to appropriate behavior that **netizens** (**Internet** citizens) observe in **virtual** communities. When you show respect for others in **email** communications, in **Web discussion forums**, or elsewhere on the **World Wide Web**, you are practicing netiquette. This chapter describes some of the conventional courtesies that responsible Internet users extend to each other.

9a General netiquette

Not all Internet forums observe the same forms of netiquette; the expectations of your audience will determine what is acceptable. For example, when using email or **real-time communication**, you may sometimes write informally, overlooking some conventions of spelling, punctuation, and mechanics. Documents published on the Web are, by contrast, perceived as more public and permanent than email or **listserv** postings and therefore require more attention to writing conventions. In particular, readers in academic communities expect Web writers to observe all the conventions of essay and research paper writing.

The following two rules of thumb apply to all Internet publications: (1) respect your readers, and (2) respect others' time.

Respect your readers.

People from all over the world communicate on the Internet. In your writing, you must often consider the needs and reactions of global audiences. Don't assume, for example, that slang, jargon, and abbreviations will be understood by everyone. Explain ideas carefully and provide contexts to help others follow and understand your points. If you disagree with someone publicly online, do so tactfully. If you must disagree strongly with someone, consider doing so by private correspondence. Don't engage in **flaming** (the public posting of personal attacks). Readers on listservs and in newsgroups find such posting offensive.

Respect others' time.

Remember that your readers value their time. When using email, make your messages easy to read and answer. For Web audiences, design your documents so that they can be downloaded quickly. When communicating in real time, use commonly known abbreviations and acronyms. Whenever you communicate via the Internet, do all you can to help others and yourself save time when reading, responding, or downloading.

For general introductions to netiquette, visit the following sites:

> *Using and Understanding the Internet*
> <http://www.pbs.org/uti/guide/netiquette.html>
>
> *The Core Rules of Netiquette*
> <http://www.albion.com/netiquette/corerules.html>

9b The World Wide Web

The **World Wide Web** connects a multitude of Internet resources by **hypertext**. Using **HTML (hypertext markup language)**, Web writers publish pages, often enhanced by graphics or audio, that typically include links to other Web pages or sites. When you publish research papers or other writing on the Web, make a point of observing the following guidelines.

Avoid plagiarism by acknowledging your Web sources.

Avoid plagiarism by clearly indicating both print and online sources for borrowed ideas, direct quotations, paraphrases, and summaries in your print or online texts. See Chapters 5–8 for specific advice on citing and documenting Internet sources.

Be aware that anyone — instructors included — can use today's fast search tools to detect plagiarism by searching the Web for texts containing identifiable strings of words from the document in question. In addition, many graphics now contain **digital watermarks** that enable Web managers to trace the unauthorized use of copyrighted images. To avoid embarrassment and more serious consequences of plagiarism, make a habit of providing accurate and complete citations for information you find on the Web.

Notify Web-site owners when you make links to their Web pages.

Although you're not required to ask permission to link to another's site, most Web-page authors appreciate a brief email message stating that you have created a link to their Web sites. Doing so helps them gauge the nature of their audience and the significance of their work, and gives them the opportunity to provide additional information. Example 9.1 (on page 138) shows how such a request might be worded.

Remember the value of your viewers' time.

For Web users who view documents with slow modems, downloading images can be time-consuming. Instead of placing very large images in HTML documents, limit the file size of the image to 20 kilobytes (KB) or create **thumbnails** (miniature images) that viewers can click on to see an enlarged version. (See 10e for more detailed advice.) When appropriate, describe file sizes when providing links. For example, if you include video, sound, or large graphics files with your text, indicate file sizes next to any file names or descriptive information (e.g., Juan Gris, *Portrait of Picasso*, 160 KB). Your readers can then estimate how long it will take to download the file.

EXAMPLE 9.1

FROM: linda@kahana.pgd.hawaii.edu
TO: engharnack@acs.eku.edu,
      phiklepp@acs.eku.edu
SENT: Friday, January 2, 1998
CC: gjtaylor@kahana.pgd.hawaii.edu
SUBJ: Request to link citation guidelines

Dear Dr. Harnack and Dr. Kleppinger,

Jeff Taylor and I have released a new educational Web journal called _Planetary Science
Research Discoveries_. It is a monthly publication written for teachers and students.
Your essay "Beyond the MLA Handbook: Documenting Electronic Sources on the Internet"
at <http://english.ttu.edu/kairos/1.2/inbox
/mla.html> is a very helpful document, and we
would like to link it to our site at <http://
www.soest.hawaii.edu/PSRdiscoveries>. May we
have your permission to do so? Thank you very
much.

Linda Martel
Education Specialist—Planetary Geosciences
University of Hawaii
linda@kahana.pgd.hawaii.edu

Include the option of text-only links in your HTML documents.

Not all Internet users desire or benefit from graphics.
Some readers skip graphics to save research time.
Others, lacking a graphic browser, are not able to view
documents containing an **image map** but no text.
Moreover, the visually impaired regularly "view" documents with devices that can read text to them. For these
audiences, provide text-only options in your HTML documents. See *The Lynx Manifesto* at <http://world.std
.com/~adamg/manifesto.html> for tips on constructing
texts that describe images for users whose browsers
don't display them.

Indicate the date of last revision.

Include the date of your last revision (preferably at the

end of the document) so readers can gauge the currency of your publication.

Keep URLs as simple as possible.

Because URLs are often long or case-sensitive, readers sometimes find them difficult to copy exactly. Keep file names and directory paths simple; use capital letters sparingly.

Provide URL information in your Web text.

Not all browsers automatically provide a document's URL somewhere on the printout. It will be very helpful to readers if you include the actual URL in the document itself, preferably after the date of publication or last revision. Readers of printouts will then be able to refer to your document's URL accurately and access its Web site.

Give readers a way to contact you.

Near the end of your publication, give readers the opportunity to send you an email message by providing a link to your own email address.

Protect your work.

Any original work created after 1978 automatically has copyright protection. However, it is good practice to protect the integrity of your Web publications with a copyright notice that includes the word *Copyright* or the symbol ©, the year of publication or creation, and the copyright holder's name, as in the following example:

▶ © 1997 Donna Hawkins

To establish a more defensible copyright for legal purposes, register your work with the U.S. Copyright Office, which offers forms and further information at <http://lcweb.loc.gov/copyright>.

Be aware of legal issues.

Writers who misuse copyrighted materials or publish obscene, harassing, or threatening materials on the Internet can violate local, state, national, or international laws and be subject to litigation. As a writer and publisher of electronic documents, you are responsible for what you allow users worldwide to access.

For more on Web netiquette, see Arlene Rinaldi, "The Net: User Guidelines and Netiquette: World Wide Web" at <http://www.fau.edu/rinaldi/net/web.html>.

9c Email

Email (electronic mail) lets you exchange computer-stored messages with others via the Internet. To your **ASCII** messages, you can attach formatted text files as well as files containing audio and graphics. When sending email, remember that its content is harder to keep private than that of **snail mail**. You can make an online communication secure by encryption (coding), but once your recipients decode it, they might, even accidentally, forward it to anyone else on the Internet. Treat every email message, even so-called private ones, as potentially public information. Although you may consider it improper, by hitting the Forward command your recipient can send your message (or part of it) to individuals, newsgroups, or listservs. Govern your use of email accordingly.

The following are widely practiced guidelines for email netiquette. (See also 2b.)

Address email carefully.

Email addresses are sometimes difficult to type exactly (e.g., the letter O is easily confused with the number 0). When sending email, enter the address with special care. If you type the address incorrectly, an "undeliverable mail" notice may not appear in your mailbox for a while, and you may not realize your error until hours or days later. The best ways to ensure accuracy are to use your address book, to copy and paste an address from a previous message, or, if responding, to use the Reply function.

Provide useful subject lines.

All email messages are delivered with **subject lines** (brief descriptions that appear in the recipient's email directory). Your subject line should provide a short description of your message's content or main point. Some readers receive many messages daily, so get your recipient's attention by making sure the subject line accurately reflects your message's content:

▶ Subject: ENG 101 MOO Schedule

While your readers may be satisfied with short descriptions of content, they may also appreciate the use of the following notices when appropriate.

Nonurgent information: If your message doesn't require a response, type "FYI:" (For Your Information:) at the beginning of the subject line:

▶ Subject: FYI: Florida Tour Travel Schedule

Time-sensitive information: When sending information that requires a quick response, use "URGENT:"

▶ Subject: URGENT: What about Florida tour?

Long messages: If the message is long, warn readers with a parenthetical notice:

▶ Subject: Complete FL Itinerary (LONG)

When replying to or forwarding a message, change the subject line if necessary.

If you change the topic when you're replying to or forwarding a message, rephrase the subject line to reflect the change in your message's content or your purpose in sending it.

Write crisp, clear messages.

Write crisply and to the point. Avoid overly long sentences. In general, make your online paragraphs shorter than those you would write for an off-line medium. Skip a line between paragraphs (rather than indenting them) to make your messages easier to read. Use numbered lists when possible. When quoting from a previous message, quote only what is necessary.

Use well-known abbreviations.

Many online correspondents use abbreviations and acronyms in informal email (and other informal messages). Box 9.1 (on page 124) lists some abbreviations that are generally acceptable in informal writing.

Use normal capitalization.

Don't send messages using all capital letters. Capitalized text is harder to read than lowercase or mixed-case text. In addition, messages composed in capital letters are said to "shout" rather than making their point through effective language. Similarly, avoid using all

---

Box 9.1
Commonly used online abbreviations

afaik	as far as I know
afk	away from keyboard
atm	at the moment
b	be
b4	before
bbiaf	be back in a few minutes
brb	be right back
btw	by the way
c	see
cul	see you later
f2f	face-to-face
focl	falling off the chair laughing
fwd	forward(ed)
hhoj	Ha! Ha! Only joking!
imho	in my humble opinion
irl	in real life
lol	laughing out loud
oic	Oh, I see!
r	are
rotfl	rolling on the floor with laughter
ttyl	talk to you later
u	you
y	why

For an extensive list of such abbreviations, see "Abbreviations &
Acronyms" at <http://www.cynet.net/abrv.html>.

---

lowercase letters; such text is also hard to read and too
informal for most situations.

Use underscore marks or asterisks to indicate emphasis.

Since most email is sent and received in ASCII unformatted text, you can't use italics or boldface text to show
emphasis. To show that text should be read as *italicized,*
place an underscore mark before and after whatever letters or words might otherwise be italicized. Another
way to show emphasis (but not specifically italics) is by
putting an asterisk before and after the text in question.

▶ Has anyone read _Moby-Dick_ lately?

▶ I have, and it took me a *long* time!

When responding, delete email headers.

If you answer a message and include that message in
your reply, trim the first message's **header** (routing

information) so that your correspondent doesn't have to read it.

Quote sparingly to establish your reply's context.

If you include portions of a previous message in your reply, quote only what is necessary to remind your correspondent what you are responding to. By Internet convention, lines included from a previous message are preceded by **greater-than signs (>)**. Some mail editors and newsreaders automatically mark quoted material with > signs at the left margin. Others require you to do it manually.

Send attachments with care.

Many email systems let you send attachments with your email messages. However, to open and read your attachments, recipients must have the necessary software. Before sending an attachment, ask your correspondent by email whether he or she can accept the attachment. If not, you can copy and paste wordprocessed material into your email message, provided the material is not very long.

Compose useful signature files.

Some email systems let you create a **signature (sig) file** that automatically appears at the end of each message you send. It might, for example, contain your full name, your email address, your homepage URL, your affiliation, and information about contacting you offline:

▶ Andrew Harnack <engharnack@acs.eku.edu>

  URL: <http://www.english.eku.edu/harnack>

  Eastern Kentucky University, Richmond, KY 40475

  Phone: (606) 622-2093 / Fax: (606) 622-1020

By including your email address in a sig file, you ensure that readers can reply to you without analyzing the message's header. Keep sig files to four or fewer lines if possible.

Edit and proofread your text.

Before sending an email message, review the entire text to make sure it clearly conveys your meaning. (This step is especially important if the text fills more than one screen; by the time you finish writing, you may forget what you wrote in the start of the message.) Ask yourself whether the spontaneity of email has led you to write anything you might later regret. Finally, proofread the text for grammar, spelling, and punctuation errors.

See "Necessary E-Mail Netiquette" at <http://198.209 .222.15/rberne/manners.htm> for more information.

9d Listservs

Listservs allow people from all over the world who share a common interest to communicate their ideas, ask questions, and develop extensive **threads** on particular topics. (See 2d.) When you join a listserv, you'll receive via email a standard letter of welcome. Thereafter, all messages sent to the group will appear in your email box. You can post messages to everyone on the listserv; you can unsubscribe (sign off) from a list at any time; and you can usually get a list of the listserv's members and their email addresses. Not all listservs are open to the public; subscription to many professional and scholarly lists is by special application. Consult *Liszt, the Mailing List Directory* at <http://www.liszt.com> for an extensive list and description of listservs.

Netiquette for listservs includes all of the guidelines for **email** correspondence (see 9c). The following advice extends email netiquette to include specific courtesies that listserv subscribers observe.

Save your letter of confirmation.

After subscribing, save your confirmation letter; it contains important information on how to send messages to the list, how to contact the **listowner**, how to suspend incoming messages if you're away for more than a day or two, and how to unsubscribe from the listserv.

Read the listserv's FAQ.

Most listservs periodically post an **FAQ** document or make one easily available to subscribers. Answers to questions about netiquette are generally included.

Lurk before posting.

After you join a list, monitor the messages for a few days to get a feel for the tone of the conversation and what topics are considered appropriate. Such **lurking** lets you get to know the group before you start posting.

Ask for private responses when appropriate.

Not all messages need go to every listserv subscriber. For example, when conducting a survey, ask that responses be sent to you personally. Once you've gotten answers to your questions (whether as public postings or as private email), post a summary of the answers to the group.

Don't clutter a listserv with well-known information.

If you provide a commonly known answer to someone's question, do so by private email. If someone posts a message that is off the subject, don't reply to the list; instead, reply by email. Private responses help minimize the number of duplicate public responses to a single question.

Delete extraneous text when responding to previous postings.

When quoting another person's message, delete parts that aren't relevant to your reply. For example, never quote an entire long message if all you add is "I agree!" When you quote selectively, be sure not to distort the other person's meaning.

Suspend mail or unsubscribe appropriately.

If you need to suspend mail for a while or unsubscribe from the listserv altogether, don't send your request to the listserv itself; instead, consult the FAQ or your confirmation letter for directions on how to suspend mail and unsubscribe.

For further discussion, see Arlene Rinaldi, "The Net: User Guidelines and Netiquette: Listservs/Mailing Lists /Discussion Groups" at <http://www.fau.edu/~rinaldi /net/dis.html>.

9e Newsgroups

Newsgroups allow you to participate online in forums dedicated to specific topics. (See 2e.) You can read messages that people have posted, respond to them, and write and send your own postings. Many of the courtesies observed by newsgroup participants are similar to those practiced in email correspondence and listserv participation (see 9c and 9d).

Read the newsgroup's FAQ.

If the newsgroup in which you're interested publishes an **FAQ** document, read it carefully. For a list of available newsgroup FAQs, see "USENET FAQs by Newsgroup" at <http://www.cis.ohio-state.edu/hypertext/faq/bngusenet /top.html>.

Lurk before posting.

Lurk — that is, read a newsgroup's correspondence — for a while before you post. By lurking, you will get a sense of the participants, their concerns, and the communication tone they have established among themselves.

Ask for private responses when appropriate.

If neither reading a newsgroup's FAQ nor lurking provides the information you need, go ahead and post. If you request basic information, ask that responses be sent to you by email so that other readers don't have to wade through screens full of identical answers.

For more on newsgroup netiquette, see "A Primer on How to Work with the Usenet Community" at <http:// nice.ethz.ch/Usenet/netiquette_engl.html>.

9f Real-time communication

1 MUDs and MOOs

MUDs (multi-user domains) are **virtual** places that allow many people to communicate in real time. **MOOs (multi-user domains, object-oriented)** permit not only real-time communication but also the creation of virtual objects (e.g., blackboards, quizzes, notebooks, tables and chairs). (See Figure 2.8, on page 43, for an excerpt from a MOO conversation.) Because of MOOs' object-building feature, some instructors and students prefer them to MUDs. Both MUDs and MOOs are widely used in educational settings. Although this section focuses on MOOs, its advice applies to MUDs as well. (See 2f.)

While there are many kinds of MOOs — social, educational, professional, and research-oriented — all MOOs encourage communication that respects other participants and MOO resources. The following netiquette guidelines represent the consensus of people who manage educational MOOs.

Respect other people.

Participants in MOOs come from a wide range of cultural, religious, and ethnic backgrounds. Many **newbies** may be apprehensive and will appreciate encouragement and advice. While freedom of speech is valued within MOOs, obscene language, harassment, unwanted sexual advances, and other blatantly offensive behavior and language are not tolerated. Those who engage in such behavior are quickly reprimanded and, if necessary, removed from the MOO.

Familiarize yourself with basic commands.

In addition to everyday language, MOOs use a variety of special commands. Before plunging into a MOO conversation, familiarize yourself with the commands of the MOO you're visiting. (For a sampling of MOO commands, visit "Basic MOO Commands" at <http://www.hunter.cuny.edu/ieli/moo-cmd.html>.)

Ask for permission to visit a person or join a conversation.

Most people visit a MOO for a specific purpose — perhaps to participate in a class discussion, confer with a teacher, read a chapter from a book, prepare a lecture, work through an assignment, socialize with friends, or work on a project with others. Instead of arriving uninvited in a room where others are present, always "knock on the door" by typing @*knock* and ask if you may join those present by typing @*join*.

Use well-known abbreviations in conversation.

MOO conversationalists have created many abbreviations and acronyms useful in real-time communication. Box 9.1 (on page 142) lists some abbreviations used in MOO sessions and in other forms of online communication.

Avoid spamming, spoofing, and spying.

To **spam** is to fill another's screen with unwanted text. To *spoof* is to display text that is not obviously attributed to you or your character. To *spy* is to **lurk** for a malicious purpose or use any mechanism that intercepts messages not intended for you. These behaviors violate the standards of courtesy expected among MOOers.

Ask for permission to record conversations.

Before recording a MOO session, obtain the permission of all other participants in that session. If you plan to distribute a transcript of a conversation by email (on a distribution list or a listserv), announce your intention to do so and get everyone's permission.

Respect the property of others.

MOOs contain virtual objects (e.g., rooms, desks, chairs, blackboards, laboratory equipment, recorders) that have been created and are owned by registered participants. Some, but not all, objects are available for public use. Don't teleport (electronically transport) an object without its owner's permission. Always ask for permission to use objects that don't belong to you; when you have finished using the objects, leave them where you found them.

Respect a MOO's resources.

When creating objects in a MOO, remember that MOO resources are limited. Poorly designed objects can affect the performance of the entire MOO. Avoid designing code or creating objects that consume large amounts of processing time or resources. Always consult your MOO's wizard, manager, or administrator before starting an extensive project. When copying or modifying someone else's code, ask permission first, and then comply with any requests that person has regarding the use of the code.

For further information about MUDs and MOOs, visit "Educational MUDs and MOOs" at <http://www.immll .uow.edu.au/Subjects/EDGA950/Lori/Educational _MUDs_%26_MOOs.html>. For more on MOO netiquette, visit "Collected MOO Manner Guidelines" at <http:// www.daedalus.com/net/manners.html> and "Expected Behavior and Manners for Diversity University MOO" at <http://moo.du.org/dumoo/manners.htm>.

2 Internet relay chat

Internet relay chat (IRC) is a multi-user, multichannel network that allows people all over the Internet to talk to one another in real time. Each IRC user or "client" chooses a nickname. Topics of discussion on IRC are as varied as the topics of newsgroups. Technical and political discussions are popular, especially when world events are unfolding. Most conversations are in English, but there are channels in Finnish, French, German, Japanese, and other languages.

The following advice describes basic IRC netiquette.

Enter and exit conversations unobtrusively.

You don't need to greet everybody on a channel person- ally; one "Hello!" or its equivalent is usually enough. Don't expect everyone to return your greeting. If you must say hello or goodbye to somebody you know, do it in a private message.

Be patient.

Instead of jumping headfirst into a conversation, **lurk** a while to get a feel for the tone of the conversation and the personalities of participants. When you do start chatting, realize you'll need to be on the same channel for quite a while (maybe several days) before others rec- ognize you as a "regular."

Use well-known abbreviations in chats.

Participants in IRC often use abbreviations to speed up communication. See Box 9.1 (on page 142) for a list of commonly used abbreviations. "Shano's Chat Acronym Database" at <http://www.shano.com/acronym> pro- vides an extensive list of IRC abbreviations and acronyms.

For more information about IRC, visit the following Web sites:

A Short IRC Primer
<http://www.irchelp.org/irchelp/ircprimer.html>

Internet Relay Chat FAQ
<http://www.irchelp.org/irchelp/altircfaq.html>

Yahoo!–Computers and Internet:Internet:Chat:IRC: Channels
<http://www.yahoo.com/Computers_and_Internet /Internet/Chat/IRC/Channels>

CHAPTER TEN

Publishing on the World Wide Web

The **Internet** provides many opportunities for publication—for example, on **listservs** and in **newsgroups** and **Web discussion forums**. Since the **World Wide Web** is the most public, most formal venue for Internet publication, this chapter focuses on the special requirements of publishing on the Web.

Composing Web pages differs in significant ways from writing and publishing in traditional print formats. Unlike printed pages, which present most information in linear fashion, Web texts dramatically expand your opportunities for creative text production and retrieval as well as incorporation of other documents, graphics, sound, and video.

10a Composing Web texts in HTML

You may have occasion to compose **hypertexts** for publication on the Web. A hypertext is a collection of documents containing links that let readers move easily from one document to another. Hypertexts may include graphics, sound, and video, in which case they are often referred to as *hypermedia*.

Hypertexts are created by formatting documents in **HTML**, a code for tagging **ASCII** texts, typefaces, type sizes, colors, graphics, and video to create **hyperlinks**. This formatting is automated by programs such as Microsoft FrontPage, Adobe PageMill, and Netscape Navigator Gold. You can also learn to construct and edit HTML code manually, a skill that is invaluable for troubleshooting and improving your Web pages. Here's the HTML text for "Zoo-MOO — MU's Educational MOO Project" at <http://www.missouri.edu/~moo>. Figure 10.1 shows the document as it appears when viewed with a graphic browser.

```
<html><head><title>ZooMOO</title></head>

<body bgcolor="#ffffff">

<table><tr><td>

<img height=125 width=137 align=left
src="moocow.gif" hspace=5 vspace=15 alt="">

</td>
```

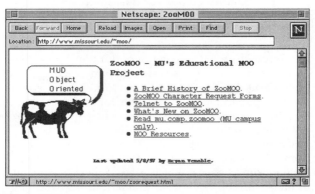

Figure 10.1
An HTML document viewed with a graphic browser
"ZooMOO—MU's Educational MOO Project," 8 May 1997, 10 Oct. 1997 <http://www.missouri.edu/~moo>.

```
<td>
<h3>ZooMOO - MU's Educational MOO Project</h3>
<ul>
<li><a href="history.html">A Brief History of
ZooMOO</a>.
<li><a href="zoorequest.html">ZooMOO Character
Request Forms</a>.
<li><a href="telnet://moo.missouri.edu:8888/">
Telnet to ZooMOO</a>.
<li><a href="news.html">What's New on ZooMOO</a>.
<li><a href="news://news.missouri.edu/mu.comp
.zoomoo">Read mu.comp.zoomoo (MU campus only)
</a>.
<li><a href="resources.html">MOO Resources</a>.
</ul></td></tr></table>
<h6 align=center>Last updated 5/8/97 by <a href
="mailto:spif@spif.com">Bryan Venable</a>.</h6>
</body></html>
```

You can find guides to composing hypertext documents both in bookstores and on the Web (by searching for HTML writing guides). Here are some of the most popular and useful guides available on the Web:

A Beginner's Guide to HTML
<http://www.ncsa.uiuc.edu/General/Internet/WWW/HTMLPrimer.html>

An introduction to using HTML and creating files for the Web, with links to additional information.

HTML Reference Manual *(Sandia National Laboratories)*
<http://www.sandia.gov/sci_compute/html_ref.html>

Provides a comprehensive list of HTML elements.

Composing Good HTML
<http://www.cs.cmu.edu/~tilt/cgh>

Version 2.0.4 addresses stylistic points of HTML composition at both the document and the Web level.

For a longer list of guides, see *Guides to Writing Style for HTML Documents* at <http://union.ncsa.uiuc.edu/~liberte/www/html/guides.html>. Continually updated to include new coding, HTML guides are useful for beginning as well as more advanced HTML writers.

Numerous software programs for creating HTML texts (known as *HTML editors*) are also available. For descriptions and evaluations, consult one or more of the following:

> *World Wide Web and HTML Tools*
> <http://www.w3.org/Tools>
>
> *Publishing on the Web*
> <http://pix.za/pix/publish.html>
>
> *HTML Editors: The Consummate Winsock Apps List*
> <http://www.kisco.co.kr/~hollobit/winsock/shtml .html>

10b Designing Web pages

Before you start designing Web pages, ask yourself the following questions:

- Who is my audience? What will my audience learn from my Web pages? How will my audience respond when reading my Web pages?
- What are my goals in designing a single Web page or a collection of pages? To inform? To persuade? To entertain?
- How does the content of my Web pages meet my goals?
- Why would somebody visit my Web pages? How do my Web pages differ from other Web pages on a similar topic?

1 Designing individual Web pages

Here are guidelines to keep in mind as you design each Web page:

- *Keep pages short.* Make the text of your document easy to scan by minimizing the need to scroll. It is usually better to create a set of short related pages that each fit on a single screen than one long page. For example, the **homepage** for *Online!* (shown in Figure 10.2)

Figure 10.2
The homepage for *Online!*
<http://www.smpcollege.com/online-4styles~help>

has links to related pages so that you can see at a glance what's available. By presenting all the important information up front, this screen allows you to immediately evaluate the Web site's topics.

- *Use appropriate formatting.* Documents created in HTML are reformatted variously by monitors with different-sized screens. Since many viewers use 13-inch monitors, avoid creating Web pages bigger than 640 x 480 **pixels**.

- *Keep paragraphs short.* Since onscreen text is often harder to read than printed text, try not to compose paragraphs that require a lot of scrolling. Whenever possible, use bulleted or numbered lists.

- *Divide long documents into logically sequenced sections.* To help readers follow your presentation of ideas in a document three or more screens long, divide the text into sections. Consider using the conventions of a formal outline (e.g., I, II, III, etc.) with appropriate subsections (A, B, C, etc.) linked to a table of contents. Such divisions not only help readers navigate your text, they also make it easier for them to cite parts of your text accurately when documenting its use as an online source.

- *Use space liberally.* Instead of indenting paragraphs, leave blank lines between them to mark their beginnings and endings. Use space around headings and graphics to create a sense of balance on the Web page.

- *Edit your Web pages.* Spell-check and proofread your Web pages carefully. A program such as Doctor HTML at <http://drhtml.imagiware.com> can perform an automatic check for you.

2 Linking Web pages

It is, of course, possible to publish traditional print texts (conventional essays or research papers, for example) on the Web. Many writers do so. When read on a screen, these texts look like traditional papers, except that they have no page divisions. When printed out, they are nearly indistinguishable from traditional manuscripts. They have obvious beginnings, middle sections, endings, and lists of references.

However, Web texts can also be very different from print texts. Unlike paper texts that follow a fixed order, Web texts can be collections of documents linked together to give readers numerous reading options. Rather than reading from beginning to end, you might, for example, view sections of a text in a variety of sequences or directions. In general, designers of Web texts rely on one or more of the following basic schemes (shown in Figures 10.3 through 10.6) to link related information:

- *Standard linkage.* In this pattern, you link your homepage to one or more documents, and documents all link directly back to the homepage. (See Figure 10.3.)

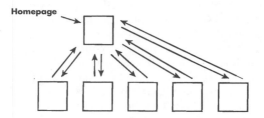

Figure 10.3
Standard linkage
Adapted from Andrew Bryce Shafran and Don Doherty, Creating Your Own Netscape Web Pages *(Indianapolis: Que, 1995) 139.*

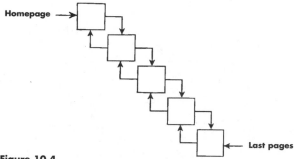

Figure 10.4
Waterfall linkage
Adapted from Andrew Bryce Shafran and Don Doherty, Creating Your Own Netscape Web Pages *(Indianapolis: Que, 1995) 140.*

- *Waterfall linkage.* In this pattern, you link documents so your readers move from one document to another in a predetermined order. Readers can only go in one direction, as if they were canoeing through a series of small waterfalls. (See Figure 10.4.)

- *Skyscraper linkage.* With this scheme, you link documents so that readers can visit sites placed two (or more) links away from the core collection of texts, but have to go back to the core to access subsequent sets of links. (See Figure 10.5.)

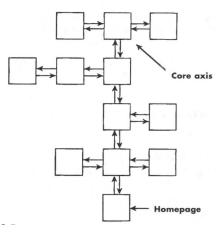

Figure 10.5
Skyscraper linkage
Adapted from Andrew Bryce Shafran and Don Doherty, Creating Your Own Netscape Web Pages *(Indianapolis: Que, 1995) 140.*

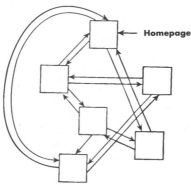

Figure 10.6
Full Web linkage
Adapted from Andrew Bryce Shafran and Don Doherty, Creating Your
Own Netscape Web Pages *(Indianapolis: Que, 1995) 141.*

- *Full Web linkage.* With this arrangement, all your documents are linked to one another so that your readers
  can visit most other documents at most other Web
  locations. This scheme works well when your collection of Web pages is moderate in size. If the collection
  is complex, this scheme may be confusing for readers.
  (See Figure 10.6.)

Many Web writers combine several of these basic patterns, so that their Web document collection may
include sections that are standard, waterfall-like, sky-
scraper-like, and/or fully webbed. How you structure
your Web texts depends on your readers' needs and
expectations, the kinds of information to be presented,
the size of documents, the complexity of relationships
among texts, and your use of graphics.

3 Using links effectively

Links let you organize information so that readers can
choose what related or supporting material to read.
Long definitions and explanations, digressions, illustrations, statistics, notes, bibliographies, and forms to be
completed—all these can be linked in separate documents to the main document.

- *Use color to highlight links to other Web sites.* Links are
  distinguished from regular text by underlining and
  color. Browsers automatically underline and color

links. If you choose link colors other than your browser's default colors, make sure the link colors contrast with your page's background color so that links stand out clearly.

- *Organize links with lists.* Using bulleted or numbered lists, group related links in logical categories.

  ▶ • Adoption
     • Transracial adoptions
     • International adoptions

- *In special instances, indicate the function of the link.* Some links enable readers to send **email**, access **FTP**, or visit **newsgroups**. When creating such links, be sure to make their function or destination obvious.

  Links for sending email. When creating a *mailto:* link, include your name and a mention of email:

  ▶ <u>Email Andrew Harnack</u>
     (in HTML: <a href="mailto:engharnack@acs.eku
     .edu"> Email Andrew Harnack</a>)

  Links for accessing FTP. FTP URLs designate files and directories accessible using the FTP protocol. When creating an FTP link, identify the action with the verb *download:*

  ▶ <u>Download Psychedelic Screen Saver</u>
     (in HTML: <a href="ftp://ftp.coast.net/pub
     /Coast/win95/scrsaver/psych20.zip"> Download
     Psychedelic Screen Saver</a>)

  Links to newsgroups. When creating a link to a newsgroup's URL, identify the newsgroup by name:

  ▶ <u>alt.adoption</u>
     (in HTML: <a href="news:alt.adoption">alt
     .adoption</a>)

- *Make links obvious and clear within larger texts.* Not all links occur within lists. When embedding a link in a sentence or paragraph, instead of inserting a marker such as *Click here,* simply make the link obvious by color and phrasing. You can assume readers know that underlined, differently colored text indicates a link. The second of the following examples communicates more efficiently than the first example. In the second example, it is obvious that **The Perseus Project** is an active link.

  ▶ The Perseus Project provides "an evolving
     digital library on ancient Greece and Rome."

For information about the Perseus Project, check here.

▶ The Perseus Project provides "an evolving digital library on ancient Greece and Rome."

- *Take care when using images as links.* When using images as links to other Web pages, use recognizable images so that readers readily understand the linkage. For example, when linking to a favorite song, use an icon that is related to music. When using a **thumbnail** (a miniature image linking to a larger version of the image), consider labeling the thumbnail if the image is hard to see. When using an **image map** (an image with areas that link to other Web documents), make the map and its sections easily understood. If possible, place text in the image to identify linkable sections of the map. For help with image maps, see *NCSA Imagemap Tutorial* at <http://hoohoo.ncsa.uiuc.edu/docs/tutorials/imagemapping.html>.

- *Keep links current.* If you create a link to a Web site that's not your own, check the link periodically to make sure it's still active. See *Site Management and Link Checking* at <http://www.softseek.com/Internet/Web_Publishing_Tools> for reviews of software designed to locate broken links.

10c Creating homepages

Your **homepage** is the HTML document in which you welcome readers to your Web site and steer them to the links and documents available at the site. Personal homepages typically include biographies, graphics, photographs, lists of links, tables, dates of construction and revisions, and the author's email address(es). Business homepages may carry logos, product announcements and reviews, links for contacting corporate representatives, and forms for making online transactions.

If you're affiliated with a college or university, find out whether it enables you to place homepages on the Web. Visit your institution's homepage to acquaint yourself with its policies regarding Web publications by students, faculty, and staff members. The homepage may also offer style recommendations and online help as well as links to research sites and to outside sites providing information on coding HTML texts. For a list

of policies and guidelines for designing some university Web pages, visit *Internet Policies and Guidelines:
Colleges/Universities* at <http://www.case.org/256
/netpol.htm>.

An excellent way to get ideas for your own homepage is to explore the work of other Web authors. For a
look at especially innovative homepage designs, visit
these Web sites:

Cool Site of the Day
<http://cool.infi.net>

Presents one attractively designed new site each day.

Personal Pages World Wide
<http://www.utexas.edu/world/personal>

Contains links to collections of personal pages at universities worldwide.

Designing effective homepages

To design effective, readable homepages, follow these
guidelines:

- Create an effective title and main heading.
- Use horizontal rules to separate sections.
- Use text highlighting (e.g., italic and bold type) sparingly.
- Use a footer at the bottom of the page for general infor-
  mation (e.g., the site's URL, a *mailto:* connection to the
  page's owner, the owner's email address) and separate
  the footer from the body of the text with a horizontal
  rule.
- Use your institution's or agency's logo where appropriate.
- Use thumbnail images as links to larger images.
- Incorporate text descriptions of images for readers
  using text-only browsers. (See 10e-3.)
- Give the date when the document was last updated.
- If the homepage is moved to a new site, leave a notice
  at the old location directing readers to the new site.

See Figure 10.7 (on page 162) for an example of an inviting homepage.

Many Web-page designers offer advice and provide
examples of their work. You may find especially helpful

Counter shows number of hits   **Table of contents indicates scope of site**
Footer gives information about page   **Rules separate sections**

Figure 10.7
Homepage for Genealogy and History of the Meldrum Family
*This Web page integrates photos, graphics, and text into a succinct,
appealing, and informative document. The hotlinks in its table of contents
allow readers to delve further into the Meldrum family's background or to
explore sites related to the broader topic of genealogy.* Ron Meldrum,
Genealogy and History of the Meldrum Family, n.d., 13 Oct. 1997
<http://www.royalriver.net/meldrum>.

David Siegel's *Web Wonk* at <http://www.dsiegel.com>
and Patrick J. Lynch's *Yale C/AIM Web Style Guide* at
<http://info.med.yale.edu/caim/manual/contents.html>.

10d Writing hypertext essays

Writing hypertext essays is similar in many ways to
composing essays for print publication. To make your
writing clear, well-organized, and persuasive in content
and style, you need to use the techniques you would use
in any type of writing. Your sentences need to be gram-
matically and mechanically appropriate. When writing

research papers and documented essays, you need to observe all the citation requirements usually associated with such publications.

In some ways, however, writing hypertext essays differs significantly from print composition. The Web offers new possibilities for communicating ideas and information: colorful graphics, background colors, video and sound, and—most important—new opportunities for organizing information. Because the Web consists of linked scrollable documents, it no longer reads—or must be read—like a book or magazine essay. Instead of turning pages or looking at the end of a chapter for notes, you can click on links to access related documents (e.g., a listing of the Works Cited). Section 10b describes some ways of organizing hypertext essays. The following guidelines suggest yet more ways to take advantage of hypertext.

- *Provide a first-page table of contents.* A first-page table of contents with links to sections of your essay allows readers to either read the essay from start to finish or go immediately to specific parts of the essay. In Figure 10.8, just below the main heading, Heather Schmocker provides links to all the sections of her essay.

Figure 10.8
An essay with a table of contents and internal links
Heather Schmocker, "Applying to Medical School," 23 Oct. 1997, 30 Oct. 1997 <http://www.arh.eku.edu/ENG/harnack/eng_301/schools .html>.

- *Use internal links in long documents.* In long single-page texts, provide internal links to various sections of the text. For example, when making a text reference to a source in your Works Cited listing, link the reference to the Works Cited entry. Then create a return link to the text reference at the end of the Works Cited entry. Always create links that allow readers to go back and forth between related sections in long documents.

- *Provide navigational links at the bottoms of pages.* When readers reach the bottom of a Web page, they may want to go to another part of the page or to a different page. Provide navigational links at the bottom of each Web document, especially if the document scrolls. Avoid dead-end pages; that is, don't create a situation where the only way to leave a page is by using the browser's Back button. Instead, provide Previous, Next, and Top-of-the-Page buttons.

10e Using images and graphics

The Internet offers a rich treasury of images, icons, graphs, charts, maps, tables, reproductions of paintings, digital photographs, and many other visuals that you can easily **download** and use to illustrate your writing or part of a Web page. This section explains how to find images on the World Wide Web and incorporate them into your work. See 10g for information on how to request permission to use copyrighted sources.

1 Finding images and graphics

With a graphic **browser**, you can visit museums such as the Louvre, view the paintings of Vincent van Gogh and Marcel Duchamp, examine architectural plans in detail, investigate mechanical drawings, peruse weather maps, enjoy film clips of rock concerts, and inspect photographs taken by the Hubble Space Telescope. The following **Web sites** provide collections of background patterns, desktop wallpaper, images, and icons that anyone can download:

Arizona State's Graphics Warehouse
<http://www.eas.asu.edu/~graphics>
Provides background samplers, a color index, and

numerous useful graphics such as arrows, balls, buttons, dingbats, and a variety of icons and lines.

The Background Sampler
<http://www.fciencias.unam.mx/ejemplo/index_bkgr.html>

Provides numerous background patterns useful for designing attractive Web pages.

The Icon Browser
<http://www.cli.di.unipi.it/iconbrowser/icons.html>

Gives access to symbols and miscellaneous icons, plus a search engine.

Multimedia and Clip-art
<http://www.itec.sfsu.edu/multimedia/multimedia.html>

A site administered by the San Francisco State University's Department of Instructional Technologies that provides links to clip art, icons, graphics, and "World Art Treasures."

Netscape: The Background Sampler
<http://www.netscape.com/assist/net_sites/bg/backgrounds.html>

Offers a wide range of backgrounds, from raindrops to stucco effects.

WebMuseum Network
<http://watt.emf.net>

Gives access to more than 10 million documents containing drawings and paintings from famous museum collections throughout the world.

Yahoo! Computers and Internet: Graphics
<http://www.yahoo.com/Computers_and_Internet/Graphics>

A useful Web page with links to clip art, computer animation, computer-generated graphics, exhibits, and software for holography, morphing, and visualization.

2 Downloading images and graphics

When you use images and graphics in Web page designs, be selective. Because it may take many minutes to **download** a large graphic, good Web-page designers use illustrations only when these deliver information in a way that the text cannot. To help your readers use their browsers efficiently, choose graphics and images that can be transmitted quickly.

The two most common image file formats in use on the Web are **JPEG** (.jpeg or .jpg, pronounced "jay-peg") and **GIF** (.gif, pronounced "jif" or "gif"). Although both formats can be used to include images in **hypertext** documents, they differ in several important ways. On the one hand, JPEG files are superior to GIF files for storing full-color or gray-scale images of "realistic" scenes such as scanned photographs. Any continuous variation in color will be represented more faithfully and in less disk space by JPEG files than by GIF files. On the other hand, GIF files work significantly better with images containing only a few distinct colors, such as line drawings and simple cartoons. For further information and advice, see "JPEG Image Compression FAQ" at <http://www.faqs .org/faqs/jpeg-faq/part1/preamble.html>.

To incorporate into your work graphics you find in other Web documents, first download the graphics to your computer and then create a link. Downloading images, graphics, backgrounds, and icons is generally easy. For example, if you're using the Netscape browser with a Windows operating system, you can download a copy of an image by using Netscape's pop-up menus. First, position your cursor over the image you want to download. Then click on the right mouse button. From the pop-up menu that now appears, choose "Save this image as," and type the appropriate information into the next **dialog box** . After you enter the information, the image will be downloaded to your computer.

If you're using a Macintosh, follow a similar procedure. Hold down the mouse button for about one second, choose "Save this image as" from the menu, and type the appropriate information into the box that appears. The image will now be quickly transmitted to your computer.

3 Integrating images and graphics with Web documents

When you use images to support textual information, choose visuals that reinforce what you say in your text, so that the visuals help your readers understand your document. Andrea Lunsford and Robert Connors in *The St. Martin's Handbook* (New York: St. Martin's Press, 1997, page 251) offer the following tips for using visuals:

- *Use tables* to draw readers' attention to particular numerical information.

- *Use pie charts* to compare a part to the whole. Use *bar charts* and *line graphs* to compare one element with another, to compare elements over time, to demonstrate correlations, and to illustrate frequency.

- *Use drawings or diagrams* to draw attention to dimensions and to details.

- *Use maps* to draw attention to location and to spatial relationships.

- *Use cartoons* to illustrate or emphasize points dramatically or to amuse.

- *Use photographs* to draw attention to a graphic scene (such as devastation following an earthquake) or to depict an object.

In short, base your choices on the purpose of your document and the needs of your audience.

When you use images in a paper or on a Web page, integrate all graphics into your text so that the images and text reinforce each other by observing the following recommendations:

- *Make readability a priority.*

- *Select background patterns that complement the subject matter of the Web page.* For example, many Web-page designers use muted and textured backgrounds that effectively foreground dark-colored textual information.

- *Choose contrasting colors for text and background.*

- *Avoid busy backgrounds.* They are distracting even when contrast is not a problem.

- *Avoid plagiarism.* Use images that are your own, that you have been given permission to use, or that are provided for anyone's use without charge.

- *Keep images as small as possible.* Crop images as closely as possible. Small files load faster and help ensure compatibility with all systems.

- *Be aware of file sizes.* Keep track of your Web page's total file size by adding up the size of your HTML file and all embedded graphics. Try not to exceed 150 kilobytes (KB) for any single complete file, because readers using a 14.4 baud modem will need to spend 1–2 minutes downloading 150KB before they can view the full page. As a rule of thumb, Web pages up to 70KB download quickly and efficiently.

- *Limit individual graphics to 20KB.* Graphics larger than 20KB often take more downloading time than many readers care to spend.

- *Resize large graphics to improve performance.* If your image is larger than 20KB, use a program such as Paint Shop Pro or Adobe Photoshop to reduce its file size. You can let readers access the original by linking the smaller image (a **thumbnail**) to a larger file. Readers can then decide whether to download the larger image.

- *Repeat use of images where possible.* Using the same image in several places helps the browser work faster because once an image is downloaded, it can be accessed quickly from the computer's local memory. It also helps to use standard bullets, bars, and banners.

- *Include text descriptions of images.* Describe images in your HTML text for readers whose browsers don't accept graphics. Users of text-only browsers see only the code [IMAGE], indicating that an image can't be displayed. Add a short ALT phrase to your HTML image tag so readers with text-only browsers see a description of the image:

  ▶ `<IMG SRC="PHOTO.GIF" ALT="Photograph of Eric Barley">`

  For information on how to insert a description of an image into an HTML document, see "The Lynx Manifesto" at <http://world.std.com/~adamg/manifesto.html> or the Help screen of your Web-page editor.

- *Provide a copyright notice.* Place the copyright symbol © at the bottom of your page to remind your readers that your material may not be reproduced without your permission.

By following these suggestions for using graphics, you will not only reinforce the content of your Web page but also present screens that are quickly loaded, easily read, and efficiently reproduced.

Using this chapter, one writer produced the Web documents shown in Figures 10.9 and 10.10.

To find more information about designing Web pages that incorporate images, visit the following sites:

Web Page Design
<http://www.uaa.alaska.edu/cas/jpc/webdesign.html>

David Siegel, *Web Wonk*
<http://www.dsiegel.com>

HTML/WWW Style Guides
<http://www.khoros.unm.edu/staff/neilb/weblint/style.html>

Memory Made Manifest: The United States Holocaust Memorial Museum

By Laura Dove

There is a link which connects the collective memory of the American people with the horror of the Holocaust. When rain soaks the ground at the sites of Auschwitz, Dachau, and other death camps, shards of bone and layers of ash work their way to the surface. This same process is at work in our recollections of the Holocaust. Americans have been unable to suppress the guilt and horror that remembering the Holocaust engenders, and have slowly come to realize that events that occurred fifty years ago and thousands of miles away demand accomodation in our national conciousness. The United States Holocaust Memorial Museum is a facet of offical American memory fitted into the iconography of the Mall in Washington D.C. This project explores <u>the nature of the Holocaust in the American consciousness</u> culminating in the creation of the Holocaust Commission in 1978, the formation and development of the <u>President's Commission on the Holocaust</u> and the U.S. Holocaust Memorial Council, and the physical and emotional parameters of the exhibit it houses.

Contents

- <u>The Holocaust in the American Imagination 1945-1978</u>
- <u>The President's Commission on the Holocaust 1978-1986</u>
- <u>The Architecture of the Holocaust Museum 1987-1993</u>
- <u>The Permanent Exhibit</u>

- <u>Producers' Bibliography</u>
- <u>Additional Sources</u>

Figure 10.9
A Web document incorporating photography
This document has links to several related documents, one of which is shown in Figure 10.10. Laura Dove, Memory Made Manifest: The United States Holocaust Memorial Museum, *n.d., 3 Dec. 1997 <http://xroads.virginia.edu/~cap/holo/holo.html>.*

The Architecture of the Holocaust Memorial

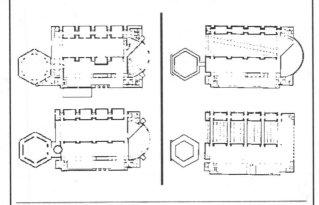

When architect James Ingo Freed accepted the commission to plan the United States Holocaust Memorial, he was nervous about the challenge of creating a building that expressed the enormity of the event. He recalled his reaction in a series of interviews with *Assemblage* magazine, saying "I have to make a building that allows for horror, sadness. I don't know if you can make a building that does this, if you can make an architecture of sensibility." In his plans for the United States Holocaust Memorial, Freed created a building of exceptional sensibility and impact. With a combination of evocative architectural language, sensitivity to the demands of his "clients" (the people of the United States, the members of the U.S. Commission on the Holocaust, and extensive government bureaucracy), and a creative approach to the requirements of the site and subject matter, Freed's building is (in the words of architectural critic Jim Murphy) "the most emotionally powerful architectural event most of us will ever experience." Freed's building utilizes the threads of American memory that undergird our conception of the Holocaust and represents an exceptionally successful architectural achievement.

With the final selection of James Freed as the architect for the memorial, the Holocaust began in earnest its quest to lend physical dimension to the horror of the Holocaust. After rejecting its initial plan to adapt existing buildings on the site, adjacent to the Mall, the commission envisaged a memorial tailored to the needs of the project and suited to the site. The building required space for a permanent exhibit, room for educational and research facilities, a place for peaceful contemplation (termed the Hall of Remembrance), and space for temporary exhibits. On October 16, 1985, the soil of the Mall was ritualistically mixed with soil from the concentration camps at the official groundbreaking. Elie Wiesel mused that, at the time, "we begin to lend a physical dimension to our relentless quest for remembrance" (Linenthal 57). For the next eight years, the planners and architects entrusted with making this memory manifest would struggle with the duty of creating a physical structure that was inclusive, unique, and evocative.

Figure 10.10
A Web document incorporating an architectural floor plan
Laura Dove, "The Architecture of the Holocaust Memorial," lkd. Memory Made Manifest: The United States Holocaust Memorial Museum, n.d., 3 Dec. 1997 <http://xroads.virginia.edu/~cap/holo/arch.html>.

10f Using video and sound

You can add audio and video enhancements to your Web documents. By coding access to small applications ("applets") into an HTML page, you enable browsers to download files containing animation, video clips, and sound effects.

1 Finding audio and video files

Many Internet archives provide collections of sound
files in appropriate formats for various platforms. For
information on finding and using audio and video files,
visit the following sites:

Using Sounds in Your Page
<http://ubmail.ubalt.edu/~abento/sounds/sounds
.html>

Soundfile Information and Users' Guide
<http://wings.buffalo.edu/epc/sound/info.html>

How to Download Graphic and Movie Files
<http://keyinfo.com/help/howto.htm>

You can find specific audio and video files at the following Web sites:

Sites with Audio Clips
<http://www.geek-girl.com/audioclips.html>

Mario's Music Links
<http://www.goldtech.com/musicpages>

Sample Audio and Video Files
<http://baretta.calpoly.edu/audio-video/samples
.htm>

2 Downloading audio and video files

Download audio and video files as you would any
file. Once you have downloaded an audio file, you may
need to change its format. "Stroud's CWSApps List—
Audio Apps" at <http://www.midwest.net/software
/cwsapps/sound.html> lists and reviews audio-format-
ting software.

3 Integrating audio and video with Web documents

Including audio and video files on your Web page provides additional ways of communicating with visitors to
the page. For example, your page can say "Welcome!" in
English or "Bienvenue!" in French; it can display the
word *Welcome!* as a rotating sign; it can play a trumpet
fanfare as your homepage downloads itself. A musicolo-

gist can include sound clips in an essay on Mozart, and film critics can show readers selected scenes from movies under discussion.

While audio and video files can add visual and rhetorical power to Web pages, keep in mind: sound that is appealing to one person can be an annoyance to another, and most video files take a long time to load and require a lot of memory. Be sure that your use of audio and/or video makes a significant contribution to your pages. Avoid filling your pages with gimmicks and features that don't look good or work well together.

10g Requesting permission to use copyrighted sources

You are free to access and read any material that is published on the Internet. Whenever you reproduce information found on the Internet, however, you are in fact disseminating that information and thus may need to seek permission to use it. Material that is copyrighted often includes a notice with the word *copyright*, the symbol ©, and the name of the copyright holder (e.g., Copyright © 1995–1997 by Benedict O'Mahoney. All rights reserved.). Such a notice indicates that the material is protected by copyright and that unauthorized use is illegal. However, even material that doesn't include a notice is likely to be copyrighted. Asssume material is copyrighted unless you know it is not.

If you want to use part or all of a copyrighted source, then you need to write to the copyright holder and request permission to use the desired text, image, or file. Examples 10.1 and 10.2 demonstrate how one might ask for permission to reproduce a copyrighted text and a graphic to be used as an illustration.

If permission is granted, then you may use the source as you have indicated. If permission is denied, however, you must respect the denial. You may, of course, create a **hyperlink** to the source itself, refer to the source, or paraphrase or summarize its contents, citing the source appropriately. If necessary, include in your paper a content note explaining your use of a particular source.

In an educational, noncommercial setting, "fair use" of copyrighted materials is allowed. Fair-use provisions in copyright law usually designate some copying as legal. The intent is to increase public access to the work

EXAMPLE 10.1

```
FROM:  stumiller@acs.eku.edu
TO:    comments@benedict.com
SENT:  Monday, January 12, 1998
CC:    stumiller@acs.eku.edu
SUBJ:  Request for permission
```

Dear Benedict O'Mahoney,

I wish to request permission to quote from "Copyright Fundamentals" on _The Copyright Website._ Quotations from your text will appear in a research paper to be submitted in my webfolio (collection of online writings). The paper will, in part, help writers do research on the Internet. I will, of course, give credit to you as the author of my source and will specify <www.benedict.com/fund.htm#fund> as the original URL. Please let me know if such permission is granted. Thank you.

Alice Miller <stumiller@acs.eku.edu>

without infringing on the benefits derived from the work by the author or publisher. Generally, fair use of copyrighted material for personal, noncommercial use is not a copyright infringement.

Laws regarding rights to intellectual property available on the Internet continue to evolve. If you need answers to questions about copyright law, permissions, and good ethical practice, turn to the Internet for up-to-date information on these subjects. The sites listed in Box 10.1 (on page 175) provide useful information.

10h Using Internet sources in hypertext essays

1 Avoiding plagiarism by acknowledging online sources

Plagiarism, defined as the fraudulent presentation of someone else's work as your own, is almost universally condemned. Nearly all style manuals explain why plagia-

EXAMPLE 10.2

```
FROM: stumiller@acs.eku.edu
TO: malick@www.acm.uiuc.edu
SENT: Friday, January 9, 1998
CC: stumiller@acs.eku.edu
SUBJ: Request for permission

Dear _____,

I am a student at Eastern Kentucky
University. I would like to request permis-
sion to download and use <escher-2worlds.gif>
as an illustration of M. C. Escher's work.
The illustration will be part of a class pro-
ject for my first-year composition course.
When using the image, I will cite <http://
www.acm.uiuc.edu:80/rml/Gifs/Escher> as the
URL, unless you specify a different credit
line. Thank you for considering my request.

Alice Miller <stumiller@acs.eku.edu>
```

rism must be avoided and how to give credit to other writers when citing their ideas or wording. Moreover, most
colleges and universities have official policies concerning
plagiarism and specific penalties for punishing offenders.
(See, for example, the "Carnegie Mellon University Policy
on Cheating and Plagiarism" at <http://infoserver
.andrew.cmu.edu/policy/documents/Cheating.html>.)

The Internet makes it easy for you to use other
sources in your writing and encourages collaboration
among its users. As a result, the traditional notion of the
"author" as a single individual working alone on his or
her document can be difficult to maintain in an online
context. Many software programs promote group writing in the form of collaborative drafting, editing, and
revision. Such "patchwriting" means that our print-
based notions about who "owns" a text—and what
exactly constitutes an *author*—must now be rethought
and perhaps redefined.[1]

---

[1] See, for example, Rebecca Howard, *Standing in the Shadow of
Giants: Plagiarism and Writer-Text Collaboration in Composition Pedagogy*
(Norwood, NJ: Ablex, forthcoming).

Box 10.1
Sites providing information on copyright issues

United States Copyright Office
<http://lcweb.loc.gov/copyright>

The Copyright Act of 1976
<http://www.law.cornell.edu/uscode/17>

10 Big Myths about Copyright Explained
<http://www.clari.net/brad/copymyths.html>

An Intellectual Property Law Primer for Multimedia and Web Developers
<http://www.eff.org/pub/CAF/law/ip-primer>

Copyright Law: Some Fundamental Sources
<http://www.iupui.edu/it/copyinfo/sources.html>

The fourth edition of the *MLA Handbook for Writers of Research Papers* by Joseph Gibaldi (Modern Language Association, 1995) recognizes that certain forms of writing often involve collaborative efforts, which the traditional guidelines regarding plagiarism do not always address:

> [One] issue concerns collaborative work, such as a group project you carry out with other students. Joint participation in research and writing is common and, in fact, encouraged in many courses and in many professions, and it does not constitute plagiarism provided that credit is given for all contributions. One way to give credit, if roles were clearly demarcated or were unequal, is to state exactly who did what. Another way, especially if roles and contributions were merged and truly shared, is to acknowledge all concerned equally. Ask your instructor for advice if you are not certain how to acknowledge collaboration. (29)

Authors of print sources commonly acknowledge participants in collaborative writing projects at the beginning of a book, essay, or research report, often in a preface or note. Internet writers, too, must acknowledge help from other authors and researchers, as well as from page designers, graphic artists, funding institutions, and software developers. In your hypertext document, you can dedicate a separate linked page to acknowledging help and sources. Example 10.3 (on page 176) shows an extract from a typical acknowledgments page.

When you engage in online composition and publication, not only do you open yourself to the possibilities of

collaboration, you also assume responsibility for acknowledging the influences that make such writing possible.

2 Citing Internet sources in hypertext essays

A hypertext essay often contains links to sources cited in
the text. For this reason, some instructors do not require
their students to append a list of works cited when they
are citing only Internet sources in an essay. If all of the
sources are already connected to the HTML text, readers
can retrieve them without a separate list.

EXAMPLE 10.3

Acknowledgments

Project Censored Canada (PCC) is very much a
collective effort. We wish to thank the journalists who wrote the underreported stories;
the magazines and newspapers that published
them; and the journalists, activists, and
other interested individuals who nominated
the stories. We also wish to thank the
researchers, students participating in PCC
seminars at both Simon Fraser University and
the University of Windsor in the spring of
1995. Our researchers analyzed approximately
150 nominations to determine if they quali-
fied as underreported stories and then
selected the top eighteen for forwarding to
our distinguished national panel of judges,
to whom thanks are also due.

Student Researchers

Diane Burgess, Laurie Dawkins, Cameron
Dempsey, Chantal Ducoeurjoly, Bill Duvall,
James Duvall, Shoni Field, David Fittler,
Rita Fromholt, Tony Fusaro, Dale Gamble,
Madelaine Halls, Clayton Jones, Ava Lew,
Cheryl Linstead, Kirsten Madsen, Lauren
Maris, Jennifer Morrison, Carmen Pon,
Elizabeth Rains, Steve Rennie, Humaira Shah,
Karen Whale, and Tracy Workman.

*"Project Censored Canada: Researching the Nation's News Agenda.
A joint project of the School of Communication, Simon Fraser University
Department of Communication Studies, University of Windsor,"
25 Apr. 1996, 26 June 1996 <http://cc6140mac.comm.sfu.ca
/acknowledgements.html>.*

Since Internet sites can easily be revised, archived, or even removed from the Internet, some instructors require a list of sources even for a hypertext essay citing only Internet sources. Such a list provides a handy summary of all the Internet sources used in the essay and demonstrates the nature and extent of the author's research. Also, readers may need to know not only the date of a posting but also the date when the writer accessed the site. Such information, while not available from linkage data contained in essays formatted in HTML, can be made available in a list of sources cited. This information can help readers determine the currency and reliability of the Internet information. For these reasons — in order to enable readers to review the scope of a writer's research and determine posting and access dates — many instructors require a list of works cited even in hypertext essays. If you are required to provide a list of Internet works cited, see Chapters 5–8 for guidelines for citing and documenting Internet sources. You are never wrong to include a list of works cited; if you're not sure of your instructor's requirements, provide such a list.

10i Publicizing your Web documents

To enable readers to find your homepage using common Internet search tools, you must register it. Since no one registration automatically places your work on the entire World Wide Web, choose a registration service that suits your needs and appeals to your intended audiences. Some but not all registration sites charge for this service. To examine sites where you can register your homepage and other publications, visit *Web Referencing Kit* at <http:// apollo.co.uk/web-kit.html>.

To speed up the registration process, have the following information ready:

- Your document's title
- A brief description of your document
- An accurate transcription of your URL (*http* address)
- A list of keywords that people searching for your site are likely to use
- A list of categories your site would fit into in an index of topics

You are now ready to register your publication with one or more search tools.

Once you have registered your homepage, people are likely not only to read your publication but also to correspond with you about it. Reply promptly to any correspondence you receive.

10j Online guides for designing Web pages

The following Web sites offer further information and advice on composing well-designed Web pages and sites:

Style Guide for Online Hypertext (*Tim Berners-Lee*)
<http://www.w3.org/pub/WWW/Provider/Style/Introduction.html>

Has information on server administration, site structure, and document organization from the creator of the World Wide Web.

The Sevloid Guide to Web Design (*John Cook*)
<http://www.sev.com.au/webzone/design.htm>

A collection of more than 100 tips on every aspect of Web design. The tips are sorted into categories such as page layout, navigation, content, and graphics.

Web Development (*John December*)
<http://www.december.com/web/develop.html>

Discusses Web-page development and describes the characteristics of effective pages.

Art and the Zen of Web Sites (*Tony Karp*)
<http://www.tlc-systems.com/webtips.html>

Simply and elegantly presents advice, truisms, and pointed questions about navigation, design, and technology.

Guide to Web Style (*Rich Levine/Sun Microsystems, Inc.*)
<http://www.sun.com/styleguide>

Gives thoughtful guidelines for creating Web pages.

Yale C/AIM Web Style Guide (*Patrick Lynch*)
<http://info.med.yale.edu/caim/manual/contents.html>

Combines traditional editorial approaches to document creation with graphic design, user interface design, information design, and the technical authoring skills required to use HTML, graphics, and text effectively in Web pages.

Guide to HTML and Web Authoring Resources (*Northwestern University Library*)
<http://www.library.nwu.edu/resources/www/#Development>

Provides links to online guides for creating Web pages.

Style Guide (*Gareth Rees*)
<http://www.cl.cam.ac.uk/users/gdr11/style-guide.html>

Presents exceptionally useful information and recommendations.

Composing Good HTML (*James Eric Tilton*)
<http://www.cs.cmu.edu/~tilt/cgh>

Discusses Web style at both the document level (describing common errors, giving basic rules of thumb, and illustrating some differences among browser displays) and the site level.

Style Guides (*Web Publisher Resources Society*)
<http://www.cs-ka.de/gerhard.renner/wpr/3200pugu.html>

Provides links to guides, tutorials, and tips for developing Web pages.

A Directory of Internet Sources

This appendix lists URLs that make good starting points for doing research in most academic disciplines and areas of professional specialization.

Because the number of Web sites grows daily, no printed list of URLs is entirely up-to-date. In addition to using this directory, remember to visit the *Online!* Web site at <http://www.smpcollege.com/online-4styles~help>, where the directory is archived and continually updated. Bookmark this Web site so that you can easily visit it.

Sources for the following list include the Argus Clearinghouse at <http://www.clearinghouse.net>, the WWW Virtual Library at <http://www.w3.org/vl>, and the 1997 supplement to *Choice: Current Reviews for Academic Libraries.*

a General reference

Blue Web'n Learning Sites Library

<http://www.kn.pacbell.com/wired/bluewebn> links you to a growing number of Internet learning sites (lessons, tutorials, and references), "especially online activities targeted at learners."

INFOMINE: Scholarly Internet Resource Collections

<http://lib-www.ucr.edu> offers links to tens of thousands of "academically valuable resources," indexed by subject and educational level.

My Virtual Reference Desk

<http://www.refdesk.com> provides links to search engines, news and weather sites, newspapers, magazines, and reference tools for every conceivable topic, from Acronyms to ZooNet.

Whatis.com

<http://whatis.com> is an online dictionary of Internet terminology.

b Accounting

ANet Bibliography

<http://www.csu.edu.au/anet/wwwbib/anetbib-wel come.html> is a subject-specific search tool from Charles Sturt University.

AuditNet: Internet Resources for Auditors

<http://users.aol.com/auditnet/karl.htm> contains "the most comprehensive list of Internet resources for auditors and accountants available on the Internet via email, FTP, and the World Wide Web."

Rutgers Accounting Web

<http://www.rutgers.edu/Accounting/raw.html> is "an accounting information retrieval system, available on the Internet for use by accounting scholars, practitioners, educators, and students."

c Agriculture

INFOMINE: Biological, Agricultural and Medical Sciences

<http://lib-www.ucr.edu/bioag> lets you browse or search for resources on all agricultural topics.

Internet Resources for Agriculture

<http://www.aglib.vt.edu/lbmhp/interag.html> is an extensive list of resources cataloged at Virginia Tech.

Internet Resources in Agriculture

<http://www.nal.usda.gov/acq/intscsel.htm> contains hundreds of annotated links "selected by the Acqui-

sitions & Serials Branch of the U.S. Department of Agriculture, National Agricultural Library."

d   Anthropology

UCSB Cool Anthropology Web Sites
<http://www.sscf.ucsb.edu/anth/netinfo.html> is a very extensive catalog maintained by the University of California–Santa Barbara.

Voice of the Shuttle: Anthropology Page
<http://humanitas.ucsb.edu:80/shuttle/anthro.html> focuses on research-oriented sites.

The WWW Virtual Library: Anthropology
<http://www.usc.edu/dept/v-lib/anthropology.html> includes links to resources for all specialties within anthropology.

e   Archaeology

Archaeology on the World Wide Web
<http://www.swan.ac.uk/classics/antiquity.html> discusses the impact of the Web on archaeology.

ArchNet
<http://spirit.lib.uconn.edu/archnet> gives links to news, museums, and academic departments.

Voice of the Shuttle: Archaeology Page
<http://humanitas.ucsb.edu:80/shuttle/archaeol.html> emphasizes sites for research.

f   Arts (performing and fine arts)

Art Sites on the Internet
<http://artsnet.heinz.cmu.edu/Artsites/Artsites.html> "provides a central access point to cultural resources on the Internet."

Internet Resources for Music Scholars
<http://www.rism.harvard.edu/MusicLibrary

/InternetResources.html> is maintained by the Eda Kuhn Loeb Music Library, Harvard University.

Visual & Performing Arts INFOMINE

<http://lib-www.ucr.edu/vpainfo.html> is a comprehensive index to Web resources.

The WWW Virtual Library: Music

<http://syy.oulu.fi/music> categorizes links by instrument, performer, composer, genre, and so on.

g Astronomy

The Astronomy Cafe

<http://www2.ari.net/home/odenwald/cafe.html> provides an introduction to astronomy and astronomical research.

The Astronomy Net

<http://www.astronomy.net> offers links for astronomy research, equipment, software, and observatories.

The WWW Virtual Library: Astronomy and Astrophysics & AstroWeb

<http://www.w3.org/vl/astro/astro.html> links the major databases for astronomical research.

h Athletics and sports

[e]ssential Links to Sports Resources on the Internet

<http://www.EL.com/elinks/sports> links you to "professional, college, and general sports information including football, baseball, basketball, and all other sports."

My Virtual Reference Desk — Sports Sites

<http://www.refdesk.com/sports.html> gives more than 100 links to major sports sites and online guides.

World Wide Web of Sports

<http://www.tns.lcs.mit.edu/cgi-bin/sports> offers a search tool and hundreds of links categorized by sport.

The WWW Virtual Library: Sport

<http://www.justwright.com/sports> has an extensive collection of links to informational, commercial, and fee-based resources.

i Biology

BioAgMed INFOMINE

<http://lib-www.ucr.edu/bioag> is a subject-specific search tool especially designed for research.

Biology on the WWW

<http://www.epress.com/w3jbio/biolinks.html> presents a very useful collection of links to major biology Web servers and webliographies.

Scott's Botanical Links

<http://www.ou.edu/cas/botany-micro/bot-linx> is a well-annotated index to resources for botany.

The WWW Virtual Library: Biosciences

<http://golgi.harvard.edu/biopages> categorizes biology resources by type of provider and by subject.

i Business and economics

Advertising, Marketing, and Electronic Commerce

<http://www.ntu.edu.sg/library/advrtise.htm> is a "comprehensive collection of resources to information on Internet-facilitated advertising and marketing, Net culture and its relation to business, promotional sites, statistical and Internet growth information, electronic commerce, media law and electronic payment, and more."

BizEc — Select Resources in Business Administration

<http://netec.wustl.edu/BizEc.html> contains links to selected resources in business administration.

Internet Business Library

<http://www.bschool.ukans.edu/intbuslib/virtual.htm> has links to news, data, and research reports on domestic and international business and trade.

Madalyn, a Business Research Tool

<http://www.udel.edu/alex/mba/main/netdir2.html>
focuses on all aspects of business administration.

WebEc—WWW Resources in Economics

<http://www.helsinki.fi/WebEc> is "an effort to catego-
rize free information in economics on the WWW."

k Chemistry

ChemCenter

<http://www.chemcenter.org> is a service of the
American Chemical Society.

Chemistry Information on the Internet

<http://hackberry.chem.niu.edu:70/0/cheminf.html>
has a very large annotated collection of links, especially
those related to chemical education.

The WWW Virtual Library: Chemistry

<http://www.chem.ucla.edu/chempointers.html> pro-
vides links to Web, gopher, and FTP sites and Usenet
newsgroups for all aspects of chemistry.

l Classics

Classics and Mediterranean Archaeology Home Page

<http://rome.classics.lsa.umich.edu/welcome.html>
collects sources on topics ranging from ABZU to
Xanten.

Internet Resources for Classical Studies

<http://www.indiana.edu/~classics/Internet/Internet
.html> is a very large collection of links sponsored by
Indiana University's Department of Classical Studies.

ROMARCH: Roman Art and Archaeology

<http://www-personal.umich.edu/~pfoss/ROMARCH
.html> serves as "the original crossroads for Web
resources on the art and archaeology of Italy and the
Roman provinces, ca. 1,000 B.C.–A.D. 700."

m Communications

Media-Link

<http://www.dds.nl/~kidon/media.html> offers links to most international media sites, including newspapers, magazines, television, and radio.

News on the Net

<http://www.reporter.org/news> is maintained by Investigative Reporters and Editors, Inc., and has a catalog of Web sites sorted by current media story.

Telecoms Virtual Library

<http://www.analysys.com/vlib>, a section of the WWW Virtual Library, contains a search tool and links categorized by subspecialty.

The WWW Virtual Library: Journalism

<http://www.cais.com/makulow/vlj.html> offers hundreds of links for broadcasting, communications, media, and news.

n Computing

INFOMINE: Physical Sciences, Engineering, Computing, and Math

<http://lib-www.ucr.edu/pslinfo.html> is a subject-specific search tool designed primarily for research.

PC Webopædia

<http://www.pcwebopaedia.com> offers "accurate, up-to-date information about personal computers."

The WWW Virtual Library: Computing

<http://src.doc.ic.ac.uk/bySubject/Computing/Over view.html> offers links to an online dictionary of computing and to the Internet Computer Index, as well as to thousands of bibliographies and technical reports.

o Earth sciences

Brock Library Earth Science Metasites

<http://www.BrockU.CA/library/research/earthsci/metasite.htm> collects "Web pages that include a comprehensive list of information and links" on earth science topics.

Consortium for International Earth Science Information Network

<http://www.ciesin.org> "specializes in global and regional network development, science data management, decision support, and training, education, and technical consultation services."

Internet Resources in the Earth Sciences

<http://www.lib.berkeley.edu/EART/EarthLinks.html> offers catalogs of links for earth sciences, planetary sciences, geography, geophysics/seismology, climatology, and oceanography.

The WWW Virtual Library: Earth Sciences

<http://www.geo.ucalgary.ca/VL-EarthSciences.html> is a catalog of resources on all areas of earth science.

p Education

EdWeb: Exploring Technology and School Reform

<http://edweb.gsn.org> helps you "hunt down online educational resources around the world, learn about trends in education policy and information infrastructure development, examine success stories of computers in the classroom, and much, much more."

NetLearn: Internet Learning Resources Directory

<http://www.rgu.ac.uk/~sim/research/netlearn/callist.htm> is "a directory of resources for learning and teaching Internet skills, including resources for WWW, email, and other formats."

The WWW Virtual Library: Education

<http://www.csu.edu.au/education/library.html> categorizes information sources by subject and permits online searching.

q   English

The English Server at Carnegie-Mellon University
<http://english-www.hss.cmu.edu> offers links to
resources for more than 10,000 texts in many disciplines.

Indispensable Writing Resources
<http://www.stetson.edu/~rhansen/writing.html>
helps you "find everything on and off the Net that you
could possibly need in writing or researching a paper,
including links to all sorts of reference material, links to
writing labs, links to Web search engines, and links to
writing-related Web sites."

Literary Resources on the Net
<http://dept.english.upenn.edu/~jlynch/Lit> is a
searchable index for English and American literature.

r   Environmental studies

EnviroInfo: Environmental Information Sources
<http://www.deb.uminho.pt/fontes/enviroinfo>
"maintains information on organizations, business, publications, online databases and software, research, and
education" for the fields of air pollution, biotechnology,
chemistry, ecology, impact and risk assessment, laws,
pollution, sustainable development, soil and wetlands,
and water and wastewater.

EnviroLink
<http://www.envirolink.org> provides "the most
comprehensive, up-to-date environmental resources
available."

The WWW Virtual Library: Environment
<http://earthsystems.org/Environment.html> includes
links to resources in biodiversity, environmental law,
forestry, and landscape architecture.

s   Ethnic studies

Black/African Related Resources
<http://www.sas.upenn.edu/African_Studies/Home
_Page/mcgee.html> lists information sites concerning

black and African people, culture, and issues around the world.

NativeWeb

<http://web.maxwell.syr.edu/nativeweb> provides a "cyberplace for Earth's indigenous peoples."

The WWW Virtual Library: Migration and Ethnic Relations

<http://www.ercomer.org/wwwvl> is a collection of links to major Internet resources provided by the European Documentation Centre and Observatory on Migration and Ethnic Relations.

† Gender studies

Feminist Internet Gateway

<http://www.feminist.org/gateway/1_gatway.html> lists resources on topics such as women's health, women in politics, women and work, feminist arts, and violence against women.

Men's Issues Page

<http://www.vix.com/men> aims "to cover the several men's movements encyclopedically."

PlanetOut

<http://www.planetout.com/pno/netqueery> presents "everything Queer on the Net."

U Geography

The Association of American Geographers

<http://www.aag.org> links you to the work of a society whose "7,000 members share interests in the theory, methods, and practice of geography."

University of Texas Department of Geography

<http://www.utexas.edu/depts/grg/virtdept/resources/contents.htm> provides information about "profes-sional associations in geography, environmental science, and cartography, as well as associations with regional or topical interests."

V   Health and medicine

The Healthcare Metropolis

<http://www.healthmetro.com> offers "links to health-related sites across the Internet, including online medical and health journals, timely industry news, clinical information, access to Medline, interactive archival databases, and industry regulatory topics."

HealthFAQ

<http:// www.healthfaq.com> is "designed for those who want to lead healthier lives and those who want to take an active role in dealing with illness, injury, and disability."

The Wellness Interactive Network

<http:// www.stayhealthy.com> provides "access to thousands of health information resources on the Internet."

W   History

Horus' History Links

<http://www.ucr.edu/h-gig/horuslinks.html> is maintained by the Department of History at University of California–Riverside.

Internet Resources in History

<http://www.tntech.edu/www/acad/hist/resources.html> is maintained by the Department of History at Tennessee Technological University.

Places on the World Wide Web for Historians

<http://www.csusm.edu/A_S/History/websites> categorizes historical resources primarily by region or country.

X   Humanities

Voice of the Shuttle

<http:// humanitas.ucsb.edu> weaves together academic, professional, and scholarly resources for humanities research.

Webliography: A Guide to Internet Resources

<http://www.lib.lsu.edu/weblio.html#Humanities>
includes links for all the humanities including architecture, art, classics, film, history, literature, music, philosophy, and theater.

The WWW Virtual Library: Humanities

<http://www.hum.gu.se/w3vl> lists resources for
humanities topics.

y International studies

Political Resources on the Net

<http://www.agora.stm.it/politic> lists "political sites
available on the Internet sorted by country, with links to
parties, organizations, governments, media, and more
from all around the world."

Public International Law

<http://www.law.ecel.uwa.edu.au/intlaw> contains
links for all aspects of international law, including the
United Nations and the International Court of Justice.

Worldclass

<http://web.idirect.com/~tiger> gives you "instant free
access and step-by-step commentary for 1,025 top business sites from 95 countries, chosen based on usefulness
to world commerce, timeliness, ease of use, and presentation."

The WWW Virtual Library: International Affairs Resources

<http://www.pitt.edu/~ian/ianres.html> categorizes
information by area, country, source, and topic.

z Languages

ESL Home Page

<http://www.lang.uiuc.edu/r-li5/esl> is "a starting
point for ESL learners who want to learn English
through the World Wide Web," featuring links for
 listening, speaking, reading, writing, grammar, and
teaching.

The Human-Languages Page

<http://www.june29.com/HLP> helps you find "online language lessons, translating dictionaries, native literature, translation services, software, language schools, or just a little information on a language you've heard about."

The WWW Virtual Library: Languages

<http://www.hardlink.com/~chambers/HLP/WWW _Virtual_Library_Language.html> offers links to book and text collections, multilingual resources, language labs and institutions, and commercial resources on the Web.

The WWW Virtual Library: Linguistics

<http://www.emich.edu/~linguist/www-vl.html> contains links to most of the professional resources on the Web and is maintained by the LINGUIST listserv.

aa Law

ABA Administrative Procedures Database

<http://iris1.law.fsu.edu/library/admin> is "developed and maintained with the cooperation and support of the American Bar Association's Section of Administrative Law and Regulatory Practice and the Florida State University College of Law."

Finding Law-Related Internet Resources

<http://www.llrx.com/extras/sources.html> contains a thorough index for all types of legal information.

Internet Legal Resource Guide

<http://www.ilrg.com> is designed to be "a comprehensive resource of the information available on the Internet concerning law and the legal profession, with an emphasis on the United States of America."

bb Libraries and information science

Internet Library for Librarians

<http://www.itcompany.com/inforetriever> is "a comprehensive Web database designed to provide a one-stop shopping center for librarians to locate Internet resources related to their profession."

Library and Information Science, Librarianship: Finding Resources

<http://www.ub2.lu.se/lisres.html> is an extensive collection of annotated links and search strategies.

LibraryLand

<http://ansernet.rcls.org/libland> is a subject guide for all librarianship topics.

PICK

<http://www.aber.ac.uk/~tplwww/e/pick.html> is "a gateway to quality library and information science (aka LIS or librarianship) resources on the Internet."

cc Literature

Internet Book Information Center

<http://sunsite.unc.edu/ibic> "represents a massive, somewhat obsessive attempt, written primarily (but not exclusively) by a single individual, to provide comprehensive coverage of a very wide range of issues and interests in the field of books."

Literary Resources on the Net

<http://dept.english.upenn.edu/~jlynch/Lit> provides access to Web sites for literature in all periods, ancient to contemporary.

Malaspina Great Books Home Page

<http://www.mala.bc.ca/~mcneil/template.htx> covers links for Web resources about the Great Books series.

dd Mathematics

A Catalog of Mathematics Resources

<http://mthwww.uwc.edu/wwwmahes/files/math01.html> is an extensive compilation of links to U.S. and international math sites.

Math Forum Internet Collection

<http://forum.swarthmore.edu/~steve/steve/mathlists.desc.html> is an annotated catalog intended "to make it easy for mathematicians and math teachers to find the resources available for their purposes."

Statistics-Related Internet Sources

<http://www.geom.umn.edu/docs/education/chance/sources.html>, part of the Chance Database project, is an annotated catalog.

The WWW Virtual Library: Mathematics

<http://euclid.math.fsu.edu/Science/math.html> has links for research and education in all areas of mathematics.

ee Nursing

Nursing and Allied Health Internet Resources

<http://www.slackinc.com/allied/allnet.htm> has an annotation page for each resource included in this extensive collection.

Nursing Internet Resources

<http://medweb.bham.ac.uk/nursing/resources/nurse-resources> "is designed to cover the resources available on the Internet for nurses."

NursingNet

<http://www.nursingnet.org> is designed to "further the knowledge and understanding of nursing for the public, and to provide a forum for medical professionals and students to obtain and disseminate information about nursing and medically related subjects."

ff Philosophy

Hippias: Limited Area Search of Philosophy on the Internet

<http://hippias.evansville.edu> is a search tool for philosophy resources.

Philosophy in Cyberspace

<http://www-personal.monash.edu.au/~dey/phil> is "an annotated guide to philosophy-related resources on the Internet, indexing more than 1,500 philosophy-related sites, over 300 mailing lists, and approximately 60 newsgroups."

Religion and Philosophy Resources on the Internet

<http://web.bu.edu/STH/Library/contents.html> "provides a selected listing of local and world-wide Internet sources for religion and philosophy," with brief annotations for each item.

The WWW Virtual Library: Philosophy

<http://www.bris.ac.uk/Depts/Philosophy/VL> offers links to resources on all aspects of philosophy and to many other detailed guides.

gg Physics

Frank Potter's Science Gems

<http://www-sci.lib.uci.edu/SEP/SEP.html> has links for all topics within physics and covers other sciences as well.

INFOMINE: Physical Sciences, Engineering, Computing, and Math

<http://lib-www.ucr.edu/search/ucr_pslsearch.html> offers a subject index for physics resources.

TIPTOP: The Internet Pilot to Physics

<http://www.tp.umu.se/TIPTOP> lists thousands of physics resources and features "the world's most comprehensive index to online physics resources."

The WWW Virtual Library: Physics

<http://www.w3.org/vl/Physics/Overview.html> categorizes physics resources by topic and by specialized field.

hh Psychology

Mental Health Net

<http://www.cmhc.com/prof.htm> offers links to "information on disorders such as depression, anxiety, panic attacks, chronic fatigue syndrome, and substance abuse, and to professional resources in psychology, psychiatry, and social work, journals, and self-help magazines."

Scholarly Psychology Resources on the Web

<http://www.psych-web.com/resource/bytopic.htm>, part of the Psych Web project, links you to sites on all aspects of psychology.

Social Psychology Network

<http://www.wesleyan.edu/spn> is "the most comprehensive source of social psychology information on the Internet."

The WWW Virtual Library: Psychology

<http://www.clas.ufl.edu/users/gthursby/psi> has links for all branches of psychology.

ii Sociology

SocioSite: Sociological Subject Areas

<http://www.pscw.uva.nl/sociosite/TOPICS> is "the Web's definitive reference for researching any subject in society."

The SocioWeb

<http://www.socioweb.com/~markbl/socioweb> has links to sociological resources and a subject-specific index.

The WWW Virtual Library: Sociology

<http://www.ixpres.com/lunatic/soc.html> collects resources on all aspects of sociology.

ii Special needs

Blindness Resource Center

<http://www.nyise.org/blind.htm> is maintained by The New York Institute for Special Education.

Indie: Integrated Network of Disability Information and Education

<http://www.indie.ca> is a comprehensive site for people with disabilities worldwide.

Kids Together

<http://www.kidstogether.org> has information and resources for children and adults with disabilities.

kk Technology and applied arts

Edinburgh Engineering Virtual Library

<http://www.eevl.ac.uk/welcome.html> has an extensive database of engineering resources with browsing and searching tools.

ICE: Internet Connections for Engineering

<http://www.englib.cornell.edu/ice/ice-index.html> provides "a broad and complete catalog of Internet-based engineering resources to [assist] engineers, researchers, engineering students and faculty, and anyone else interested in finding this kind of information on the Internet."

The WWW Virtual Library: Engineering

<http://arioch.gsfc.nasa.gov/wwwvl/engineering.html> offers links to resources on all aspects of engineering.

ll Theater

Gravel Walk to Theatre on the Net

<http://www.oden.se/~pferm/gravel.htm> is a "really useful research directory, with assorted and explained links for everybody interested in theatre."

McCoy's Guide to Theatre and Performance Studies

<http://www.stetson.edu/departments/csata/thr_guid.html> is an extensive, annotated list for all theatrical and performance topics.

Playbill Online Presents Theatre Central

<http://www1.playbill.com/cgi-bin/plb/central?cmd=start> is "the largest compendium of theatre links on the Internet."

The WWW Virtual Library: Theatre and Drama

<http://www.brookes.ac.uk/VL/theatre> contains "a broad range of resources across the world: professional, academic, and recreational."

mm Writing

ESL Home Page

<http://www.lang.uiuc.edu/r-li5/esl> is "a starting point for ESL learners who want to learn English through the World Wide Web," featuring links for listening, speaking, reading, writing, grammar, and teaching.

The Everyday Writer: Writing Sites

<http://www.smpcollege.com/everyday_writer/wrisit.html> has links to general reference tools and sites specifically aimed at helping teachers and all writers.

Inkspot: Writing-Related Resources

<http://www.inkspot.com> is "a comprehensive resource for writers [that] includes articles, interviews, market information, discussion forums, a free writers' classifieds, research tips, and a guide to the best resources for writers on the Net."

Online Resources for Writers

<http://webster.commnet.edu/writing/writing.htm> features links to online reference tools, ezines, and grammar and style sites.

Index

Bookmarks

Use these pages to record information about useful-looking Web sites you read or hear about.

TITLE

URL

WHAT'S THERE

TITLE

URL

WHAT'S THERE

TITLE

URL

WHAT'S THERE

TITLE

URL

WHAT'S THERE

TITLE

URL

WHAT'S THERE

TITLE

URL

WHAT'S THERE

TITLE

URL

WHAT'S THERE

TITLE

URL

WHAT'S THERE

TITLE

URL

WHAT'S THERE

TITLE

URL

WHAT'S THERE

TITLE

URL

WHAT'S THERE

TITLE

URL

WHAT'S THERE

TITLE

URL

WHAT'S THERE

TITLE

URL

WHAT'S THERE

TITLE

URL

WHAT'S THERE

TITLE

URL

WHAT'S THERE